The Power Bowl

— RECIPE BOOK —

140 NUTRIENT-RICH DISHES FOR MINDFUL EATING

BRITT BRANDON, CFNS, CPT

Avon, Massachusetts

Published by
Adams Media, a division of F+W Media, Inc.
57 Littlefield Street, Avon, MA 02322. U.S.A.
www.adamsmedia.com

ISBN 10: 1-5072-0058-7
ISBN 13: 978-1-5072-0058-2
eISBN 10: 1-5072-0059-5
eISBN 13: 978-1-5072-0059-9

Printed in the United States of America.

10 9 8 7 6 5 4 3 2 1

Library of Congress Cataloging-in-Publication Data

Brandon, Britt, author.
The power bowl recipe book / Britt Brandon, CFNS, CPT.
Avon, Massachusetts: Adams Media, 2017.
Includes index.
LCCN 2016036836 (print) | LCCN 2016047517 (ebook) | ISBN 9781507200582 (pb) | ISBN 1507200587
(pb) | ISBN 9781507200599 (ebook) | ISBN 1507200595 (ebook)
LCSH: Natural foods. | Cooking (Natural foods) | Health. | LCGFT: Cookbooks.
LCC TX369 .B735 2017 (print) | LCC TX369 (ebook) | DDC 641.3/02--dc23
LC record available at https://lccn.loc.gov/2016036836

Cover design by Stephanie Hannus.
Cover and interior photography by Kelly Jaggers.

This book is available at quantity discounts for bulk purchases.
For information, please call 1-800-289-0963.

DEDICATION

I dedicate this book to my wonderful family,
with whom I look forward to spending many
more happy, healthy years!

Contents

INTRODUCTION

Are you looking for satisfying meals that are free of empty calories?

Do you want to prepare versatile dishes that are packed with necessary nutrients?

Are you having trouble finding time to prepare recipes that are quick, easy, and good for you?

Enter the power bowl.

Taking the culinary world by storm, these hardworking meals are perfect for anyone looking to combine healthy eating with delicious cuisine. And, with healthy ingredients like fresh fruits and vegetables, creamy yogurts, and crunchy nuts and seeds that add a wide variety of flavors and textures to every bite, these power bowls provide a satisfying feast for the eyes as well as the stomach.

Throughout *The Power Bowl Recipe Book* you'll learn everything you need to know about creating your own power bowls, from the kitchen necessities you need to have on hand to the health benefits of these nutritional powerhouses. The book is organized by the health benefit of each type of bowl, so you'll be able to focus your meal on a particular benefit you hope to reap. Whether you're looking for something quick to eat pre-workout, want to improve your skin, ensure a healthy heart, lose weight, and more, with these power bowls, you're well on your way to total health. And so you know what you'll get from each meal, each of the 140 recipes in this book contains "power sources," or information that outlines the essential nutrients and benefits that each recipe provides. These power sources will also help you choose the right ingredients for your own personal needs when you decide to stray from the recipes and build your own power bowls from the ground up.

Light, bright, full of flavor, and packed with essential vitamins, minerals, antioxidants, healthy proteins, carbohydrates, and fats, these power bowls provide health-boosting nutrition in every flavorful bite. So get out your bowls and make your meals work for you!

CHAPTER 1

Power Bowl Basics

So what exactly is a power bowl? What are the benefits? What exactly do you need to put a power bowl together?

If you're not familiar with power bowls, don't worry. From the benefits of healthy eating to the hardware you need to have on hand to how to store your nutrient-rich ingredients and plan out what you want for the week, in this chapter you'll learn everything you need to pull together a delicious dish that makes fueling your body easy. Let's take a look.

What Is a Power Bowl?

Power bowls are delicious, nutrient-dense, complete meals served in a single bowl. And when it comes to these healthy bowls, delicious and nutritious do not have to be mutually exclusive. Combining a variety of powerful superfoods that taste great and provide the body with a wide variety of essential nutrients, power bowls make eating healthy meals simple, easy, and delicious. Layers upon layers of sweet and savory ingredients fill each bowl with perfectly satisfying flavors and textures, making every power bowl an easy-to-create dish that leads to better health. Whether your ideal combination improves the health of your skin or safeguards your bones, brain, or heart, these combinations of nutritious foods provide powerful results that tempt the taste buds and satisfy the stomach. And with little time required to create these hardworking dishes, these easy-to-assemble meals can be eaten at home or on the go so you can satisfy your hunger anywhere, anytime.

The Importance of Plating

With fast preparation and cooking times, every power bowl gives you a quick, healthy meal packed with all-natural whole foods like whole grains, lean proteins, delicious fruits and vegetables, and spices and sauces. These dishes also provide your body with essential vitamins, minerals, and antioxidants that safeguard against illness and disease while promoting optimal health. And, unlike the average plated meal, a power bowl organizes each ingredient in layers, which means that each bite optimizes taste and texture and appeals to the eyes, making every scrumptious bite satisfying and nourishing. From beginning to end, the sensational tastes of whole, nutritious foods make every power bowl experience a delicious one!

Layer Your Ingredients

So how should you layer your ingredients to create the perfect power bowl? And what ingredients do you need to include? The health benefits of any power bowl can be attributed to the nutrition of each power source (found at the beginning of each recipe) that's included in the dish. Luckily, the foods that make every recipe nutritious are also delicious when combined with other power source ingredients. The unique combinations that make up the layers of grains, vegetables and fruits, lean protein sources, healthy fats, and delectable additions help to make every power bowl as healthy and nutritious as possible for both the body and mind. For an idea of the power sources that should be easily added to any power bowl, consider these options:

GRAINS

Offering complex carbohydrates, amino acids, and vitamins and minerals that can provide energy, improve mental clarity, and boost immune system functioning, the grains that can be used for power bowls include:

- Barley
- Brown rice
- Oats
- Quinoa
- Rice noodles
- Whole-grain pastas

Whether you opt for gluten-free dietary choices or not, the grain options available for each power bowl recipe are astounding.

VEGETABLES

Packed with unique phytochemicals that promote the health of the body's cells, tissues, organs, and systems, a variety of vegetables can be incorporated into any power bowl for a delicious and nutritious meal or snack, including:

- Beets

- Bell peppers
- Cucumbers
- Greens (like spinach, kale, and romaine)
- Potatoes
- Squash
- Tomatoes

These are just a few of the delicious vegetable options that can be combined in any power bowl to intensify flavors and improve nutrition content.

FRUITS

The fruits added into the power bowl recipes throughout the book make for antioxidant-rich breakfasts, lunches, dinners, and snacks that not only tantalize the taste buds but also promote and preserve the health of every aspect of the body. The brain, heart, bones, and digestive system all benefit from the fiber-rich fruit additions to any power bowl recipe. Some fruits that help ensure these benefits make it into your bowl include:

- Apples
- Berries
- Cantaloupe
- Citrus
- Kiwis
- Mangoes
- Papaya
- Pears
- Watermelon

The sweet addition of fruit not only adds intense varieties of flavors that can vary any dish, but also provides an assorted provision of nutrients that help everything from respiratory illnesses to blood sugar levels and cleansing of the digestive system.

PROTEINS

Lean protein sources can and should be included in every power bowl recipe for the essential provisions of not just protein but also healthy amino acids, vitamins, and minerals that improve energy, stamina, and muscle contractions. Some lean proteins that you want to consider using include:

- Beef
- Chicken
- Kefir
- Milk
- Tempeh
- Tofu
- Turkey
- Yogurt

Choose your favorite proteins and adjust every power bowl to the unique needs and preferences of your choosing.

FATS

Fats have a bad reputation for contributing to weight gain and chronic health issues, but healthy fats actually help contribute to your overall health. While supporting the health of your brain, heart, and digestive system, healthy fats can add texture, flavor, and health-boosting elements to any power bowl recipe. Some healthy fats that you should consider adding to your power bowls include:

- Avocado oil
- Coconut oil
- Flaxseed oil
- Olive oil
- Plant- and protein-based fats (such as those found in avocados, nuts, and fish)

These oils not only add creaminess to your favorite dishes, but they also provide nutrients such as omega-3 and omega-6 fatty acids that benefit the body and brain.

ADDITIONS

Adding creamy, crunchy textures to your power bowls not only improves your sensory experience while eating, but it can also improve the health benefits each bowl provides. Common bowl additions include:

- Nut milks: almond milk, cashew milk
- Nuts: almonds, walnuts, and cashews
- Seeds: pumpkin, sesame, flaxseed, and chia seeds
- Soy- and tofu-based creams

All of these additions can improve the protein, amino acids, and vitamins, minerals, and antioxidant benefits in every power bowl to provide superior cell health protection against oxidative damage from free radicals—all while making every bite of your power bowl a smooth, creamy, or crunchy flavor explosion.

SAUCES AND SPICES

No matter the benefit you want to gain from your perfect power bowl, you want to include sauces and spices that will make your bowl's flavor profile absolutely perfect. Some spices to considering including:

- Cardamom
- Cayenne
- Cinnamon
- Garlic
- Ginger
- Paprika
- Turmeric

Depending on the spices you use, these added ingredients can ensure that your power bowl has anti-inflammatory or metabolism-boosting benefits, but no matter which spice you chose, the addition of spices will take your power bowl experience to new heights. By making every bite of every bowl an exciting experience that improves overall health, delicious spices pretty much demand a spot in your dish.

KNOW YOUR INGREDIENTS

Once you have a handle on what your favorite ingredients are, you'll find that the preparation of any breakfast, lunch, dinner, or snack power bowl can be quickly and easily accomplished. So whether you're craving a creamy Apple-Cinnamon Oatmeal with Walnut Cream Bowl (see recipe in Chapter 2) breakfast filled with oats, almond milk, walnuts, apples, and cinnamon as the perfect satisfying selection, or a light and enticing Oriental Chicken Salad with Mandarin Dressing (see recipe in Chapter 6) entrée packed with lean grilled chicken in a sweet-tart mandarin orange–cranberry vinaigrette layered over a bed of quinoa and spinach, each power bowl combines delicious ingredients that make every layer a complement of the next. This easy and delicious way to prepare your food makes every meal and snack a flavorful experience that makes achieving better health easier—and more delicious—than you ever dreamed!

Benefits of Power Bowling

You now know how to create a power bowl, but why are we eating these delicious dishes in the first place? There are many benefits that can result from consuming power bowls throughout the day. For example, your daily diet is more satisfying, your body is provided with immense essential nutrition, and eating is a more simplified process, which makes mealtimes more enjoyable, and more!

Power Bowls Are Fast and Easy

It's tough to stick to eating a healthy diet if you feel that you're constantly in the kitchen preparing food. Fortunately, power bowls are clean, natural power sources that can be prepped ahead for easy-to-execute daily meal plans. By simply selecting the most appealing recipes for overall health improvement or a specific condition, it's so easy to make a simple shopping list for the ingredients needed, collect every superfood needed for the week in one grocery trip (as discussed later in this chapter), and prepare the ingredients for easy power bowl configurations that take only minutes to create. Fast and easy, the power bowl makes mealtime a delicious event that offers a healthy alternative to fast-food options and take-out alternatives.

Power Bowls Are Portable and Convenient

Between daily to-do's, work, family, and general activities, its no wonder that the average person opts for take-out or fast-food meals and snacks on a regular basis. Fortunately, power bowls are convenient to eat and easy to take with you when you're on the go. Think about it: Each power bowl is plated in one simple dish that you can throw a cover on and take almost anywhere! A power bowl and a spoon or fork are all you need to enjoy your favorite meals and snacks on a schedule that works for you.

Power Bowls Are Nutritious

With a growing percentage of the population turning to natural, holistic approaches to healing, whole "clean" foods that can naturally optimize health have become a staple for millions. With antioxidants that protect cells from free-radical damage and prevent cancerous changes in the cells, tissues, and organs throughout the body, superfoods—like those used in each and every power bowl—have become increasingly popular. And these superfoods, like bell peppers, berries, spinach, and nuts, do more than just taste good. They also:

- Improve immunity
- Boost brain health
- Cleanse the cardiovascular system
- Promote total body health and mental well-being
- Strengthen the cardiovascular system
- Strengthen the musculoskeletal system
- Detoxify the liver
- Cleanse the gallbladder
- Prevent dangerous cellular changes
- Clear the blood of damaged cells
- Improve stamina
- Sharpen mental focus
- Increase energy
- Improve mood
- Improve sleep quality

In addition, these super greens, berries, melons, and a wide variety of fruits and vegetables can easily help you "eat the rainbow," because superfoods come in all colors. This easy eating strategy of creating a rainbow-colored assortment of food on your plate is being recognized for its health-changing potential, because you're sure to get an abundance of vitamins, minerals, and unique phytochemicals in your diet if you eat the rainbow.

With intense flavors that combine to create scrumptious snacks and magnificent meals, superfoods act as power sources for life-changing nutrition that can be easily consumed in every delicious power bowl recipe.

Power Bowls Help You Eat for Specific Health Needs

One of the perks of a power bowl is that it can be tailored to provide benefits where they're needed the most. The superfoods found in each bowl can work together to help you lose weight, build strong bones, gain amazing skin, strengthen your immune system, and more! The dishes given in the recipe chapters in this book are set up to make this benefit clear, but you can use the power source information at the beginning of each recipe to see what benefit each superfood ingredient brings to the table and then use those ingredients wisely to make sure you're getting the most out of your bowls.

Make Power Bowl Prep Easy

The attractiveness of power bowls doesn't end with the delicious nutrition provided by the carefully selected ingredients. The ease and simplicity of preparing each bowl makes these meal options even more convenient and easy to adopt. And to make these bowls as easy as possible to prep, make, and store, you need to know some shortcuts. With these quick tips, anyone can enjoy the healthful power bowl system!

Ingredients (Must-Have Kitchen Staples)

As you know, the stars of every power bowl are the superfoods that add essential nutrition to each dish. Be sure to have some superfoods in your home at all times so you don't reach for fast foods instead.

Grains, greens, fruits, creamy additions, and spices can all be purchased from the average grocery store and added to your pantry, making the planning for power bowls as simple as a quick trip to the store. Whether these ingredients are fresh, frozen, dried, or canned, the average week's meals' ingredients can be selected and stored for quick prep of any morning, afternoon, or evening power bowl snack or meal.

Kitchen Hardware

Unlike some meal plans where you need to buy expensive gadgets or special pots and pans, power bowl preparation requires nothing more than the staple kitchen hardware that you probably already have in your drawers and cupboards. You'll need to have the following on hand:

For Peeling, Chopping, Slicing, and Dicing
- Colander
- Cutting board
- Paring knife (sharp)
- Spiralizer
- Vegetable peeler

Cooking Utensils
- Baking sheet
- Large pot
- Sauté pan
- Small pot

For Storage
- Plastic or glass containers
- Storage bags
- Transportable bowls

These storage containers make for quick storage of premeasured ingredients and even easier overnight preparation of power bowls that require marinating or simply need to set up overnight while you sleep.

By stocking your kitchen with tools you'll likely need, as well as some that offer unique preparation techniques, such as a spiralizer, you can prepare and create delicious and nutritious power bowls for every meal and snack throughout the day.

Shop and Prep

Whether you choose to incorporate power bowls for every meal or snack, or alternate throughout the day and week, a schedule and some prep work can make pulling together a week's worth of recipes unbelievably easy.

MAKE A LIST

Pull together a detailed list of ingredients that you need and try to buy them in a single grocery trip that will satisfy the needs for a whole week's meal preparation. Grouping your list into categories such as fresh foods, frozen foods, and canned and dry foods makes navigating the grocery store a breeze. Whether your list is comprised of mostly fresh ingredients or a combination of multiple packaged, fresh, and frozen options, the grocery list prepared from your week's meal plan cuts down on the time, cost, and craziness of the average shopping trip.

When you're at the store, follow your list and buy only what you need. You're better off walking the perimeter of the grocery store where you'll find the majority of the fresh and frozen items you'll need for your power sources. With the proper planning, anyone can enjoy a faster grocery trip.

STORING

When prepping and storing your power bowl ingredients, keep in mind that freshness is key. Onions, greens, and fruits and vegetables can be prepped, measured out, and stored in containers so you can quickly grab what you need to assemble a bowl. Even frozen ingredients can be thawed ahead of time and stored in a container in the refrigerator to allow for faster meal prep.

Again, the simplicity of the power bowl not only improves health but saves time.

Final Power Bowl Tips to Remember

To make the production of your power bowls even easier, the following tips can help guide you in the right direction (and help you avoid the wrong direction) when selecting ingredients, planning and prepping your meals, and structuring your most effective, healthy meal plans.

Opt for Organic and Avoid GMOs

Especially when selecting fresh produce and dry grains, opt for organic and non-GMO varieties that contain no chemicals or synthetic additives that can complicate or aggravate your body's systems.

Look for Local Fare

Purchasing produce from local sources such as fruit stands and farmers' markets ensures the freshness and sustainability of your power bowls' power sources. These local ingredients also last longer for extended preservation of freshness and nutrient content and quality.

Use Fresh or Frozen Foods

Fresh produce and frozen alternatives can have comparable nutrient content, so both make for healthy options for the fruit and vegetable components of your power bowls.

Pass on Packaged and Processed

While using canned or boxed rices, beans, and vegetables can make the preparation of your power bowls quicker, consider the sodium content, additional sugars, or preservatives when choosing these options. Avoid those foods that may contain additives, excessive sodium, and unhealthy preservatives and opt instead for organic varieties, low-sodium alternatives, and items with short ingredient lists. Using these types of foods can help preserve the optimal nutrition content of each power bowl.

Try New Things

If you've never used ingredients such as turmeric, ginger, or even coconut oil in your food preparations, consider them as exciting flavorful adventures that can add color and spice to every power bowl ingredient. Adding unique nutrients such as phytochemicals that combat inflammation and free-radical damage, the inclusion of new ingredients can expand your palate while also improving your overall health.

Eat What You Like

When you first get into preparing and eating power bowls, use base options that most appeal to you. Then you can gradually add other ingredients you might not be familiar with. This way you can get used to eating power bowls and design a healthy meal plan that you'll be more likely to follow and stick with.

Make Munching Mindful

Set a certain amount of time aside for each meal and snack. Include five or six daily meals and snacks in every day's meal plan, and give yourself enough time to enjoy the tastes, textures, and nutritional benefits of each meal.

With the delicious and nutritious recipes that make up the following chapters, you can enjoy countless combinations of healthy foods that give you fast, easy, and delightful ways to eat better, feel better, and live better—naturally!

CHAPTER 2
Preworkout/Energy Bowls

If you're looking for a bowl recipe that powers up your workout, you're in the right place! The recipes in this chapter—from the Sweet Potato Pie Smoothie Bowl to the Grilled Chicken Salad with Crunchy Quinoa—are packed with energizing ingredients that support every energy-related activity with clean, natural, delicious nutrition.

Each of these power bowl recipes are rich in proteins like chicken, tofu, and lean beef; complex carbohydrates like quinoa, polenta, and barley; vitamins like A, Bs, C, D, E, and K; minerals like iron, magnesium, potassium, calcium, and zinc; and low-glycemic fruits and vegetables that support energy maintenance for hours. These power sources work together to provide supportive benefits to the cells, tissues, and systems involved in energy production and produce lasting energy that will keep your mind sharp and your body moving throughout your workout.

These power bowl recipes make eating for energy an easy and delicious part of the day—every day!

Spicy Vegetable Frittata Scramble Bowl

Prep Time: 10 minutes | **Cook Time:** 20–25 minutes | **Serves 1**

2 tablespoons extra-virgin olive oil, divided

¼ cup seeded and chopped red bell pepper

¼ cup seeded and chopped green bell pepper

¼ cup peeled and chopped Vidalia onion

½ cup torn spinach leaves

3 large eggs, beaten

½ teaspoons cayenne

½ cup cooked quinoa

1 Preheat oven to 400°F.

2 Coat a 10" cast-iron skillet with 1 tablespoon olive oil and heat on the stovetop over medium-high heat.

3 Sauté red and green bell peppers and onions for 5 minutes or until cooked through, then add spinach to skillet and allow to wilt for 1 minute. Remove all ingredients from skillet and set aside.

4 Coat skillet with remaining 1 tablespoon olive oil and return peppers, onions, and spinach to the pan.

5 Pour beaten eggs over top and sprinkle with cayenne.

6 Cook in preheated oven for 10–15 minutes or until cooked through.

7 Pour quinoa into a serving bowl and top with frittata mixture. Serve hot.

PER SERVING   Calories: 499 | Fat: 28.1 grams | Protein: 25.0 grams | Sodium: 235 milligrams | Fiber: 5.9 grams | Carbohydrates: 33.3 grams | Sugar: 7.4 grams

POWER SOURCES

EGG: protein encourages of muscle repair and energy production

BELL PEPPER: vitamin C and carotenoids provide improved immunity

SPINACH: iron and vitamin K supports blood and bone health

ONION: quercetin helps to safeguard cells against free-radical damage

❋ POWER BOWL PRIORITIES

Prior to preparing a meal, visualize healthy portion sizes and take those measurements into account when preparing foods. Appropriate single-serving sizes are:

- Dairy: 1 serving is equal to 1 cup of milk or yogurt or 1 ounce of cheese
- Meat: 1 serving is equal to 3 ounces of chicken, beef, pork, or fish; comparable to the size of your fist or a deck of playing cards
- Vegetables: 1 serving is equal to 1 cup of raw, leafy greens or ½ cup cooked vegetables
- Fruits: 1 serving is equal to 1 medium-sized fruit or ½ cup sliced fruit

Apple-Cinnamon Oatmeal with Walnut Cream Bowl

Prep Time: 10 minutes | **Cook Time:** 5 minutes | **Serves 2**

1 cup shelled walnuts

2 cups vanilla almond milk

3 teaspoons cinnamon, divided

2 tablespoons honey

2 cups quick-cooking oats

1 large apple, peeled, cored, and chopped

POWER SOURCES

APPLE: natural sugars and fiber combine to calm hunger cravings and keep you feeling full

OATS: fiber supports blood-sugar-level maintenance for sustained energy

WALNUTS: omega-3, -6, and -9 support energy production

HONEY: natural sugars prevent low blood sugars during exercise

1 In a blender, combine the walnuts, almond milk, 2 teaspoons cinnamon, and honey. Blend on high until completely emulsified.

2 Transfer blender's ingredients to a small pot over high heat and bring to a boil. Remove from heat.

3 Add oats to heated cream mixture and stir. Allow to set for 5 minutes.

4 Pour 1 cup oatmeal into each of two small bowls. Top each bowl with half the chopped apples and ½ teaspoon cinnamon. Serve hot.

PER SERVING   Calories: 854 | Fat: 38.1 grams | Protein: 19.8 grams | Sodium: 166 milligrams | Fiber: 16.3 grams | Carbohydrates: 113.2 grams | Sugar: 46.8 grams

Sweet Potato Pie Smoothie Bowl

Prep Time: 15 minutes | **Cook Time:** N/A | **Serves 2**

- ½ cup shelled walnuts
- 2 cups unsweetened almond milk
- 2 teaspoons cinnamon
- 2 teaspoons ground ginger
- 3 tablespoons maple syrup
- 1 large peeled, cubed, and baked sweet potato,
- ½ small avocado, peeled and pitted
- 1 cup ice
- 1 teaspoon ground nutmeg

POWER SOURCES

WALNUTS: antioxidants support healthy metabolic functions of cells

CINNAMON: aromatic fragrance stimulates senses

AVOCADO: natural fats aid in the processes related to energy production

1. In a large blender combine walnuts and almond milk and blend on high until nuts are completely broken down, about 1–2 minutes.
2. Add cinnamon, ginger, and syrup and blend on high until all ingredients are combined, about 1 minute.
3. Add sweet potato and avocado and blend on high until all ingredients are thoroughly combined, about 1 minute.
4. Add ice gradually while blending on high and blend until smooth, about 1 minute.
5. Pour the smoothie mixture equally into each of two small bowls. Then top each bowl with ½ teaspoon nutmeg.
6. Serve immediately to prevent avocado from oxidizing.

PER SERVING   Calories: 390 | Fat: 23.2 grams | Protein: 6.6 grams | Sodium: 195 milligrams | Fiber: 7.4 grams | Carbohydrates: 40.9 grams | Sugar: 21.2 grams

☀ POWER BOWL PRIORITIES

Gingerroot contains unique oils such as gingerol and shogaol that provide the body with immense benefits to the immune system, brain, blood, and cells. This means that including it in your favorite power bowls boosts both the flavor and the health benefits of your dish. Powdered varieties of ginger are comparable to gingerroot, which makes powdered ginger a convenient option that can be easily stored for use whenever you choose.

Berry-Chutney Chicken with Spicy Greens

Prep Time: 30 minutes | **Cook Time:** 38 minutes | **Serves 2**

2 (4-ounce) chicken breasts

1 cup blueberries

1 cup raspberries

½ cup orange juice

1 tablespoon olive oil

1 cup kale

2 cups spinach

1 teaspoon salt

½ teaspoon cayenne

1 cup prepared quinoa

1 tablespoon honey

POWER SOURCES

BERRIES: anthocyanins support immunity

CAYENNE: adds antioxidants, vitamins, and minerals that help to boost metabolism

GREENS: vitamins A, C, E, and K promote cardiovascular health

1 Preheat the oven to 350°F and place the chicken in a 13" × 9" pan; set aside.

2 In a small saucepan over medium heat, combine blueberries, raspberries, and orange juice. Simmer until sauce reduces to a slightly thicker sauce, about 5 minutes.

3 Pour the sauce over the chicken breasts and bake for 25–30 minutes or until juices run clear. Remove from heat and set aside.

4 Coat a small skillet with olive oil and heat over medium heat. Then add kale and cook for 3–5 minutes or until wilted. Remove from heat and add spinach to kale. Toss to combine until all greens are thoroughly wilted, about 3 minutes.

5 Sprinkle greens with salt and cayenne.

6 Place ½ cup quinoa into each of two serving bowls. Top each bowl with 1 chicken breast and half the chutney mixture. Add half the greens to each bowl and drizzle each bowl with ½ tablespoon honey. Serve hot.

PER SERVING   Calories: 404 | Fat: 7.1 grams | Protein: 31.2 grams | Sodium: 906 milligrams | Fiber: 9.6 grams | Carbohydrates: 54.8 grams | Sugar: 25.0 grams

Chipotle Chicken with Polenta

Prep Time: 10 minutes | **Cook Time:** 25 minutes | **Serves 2**

2 tablespoons olive oil, divided

2 (4-ounce) chicken breasts, halved lengthwise

1 teaspoon salt

2 chipotle peppers, seeded and sliced

1 small green bell pepper, seeded and sliced

½ small yellow onion, peeled and sliced

1 cup spinach

2 cups prepared polenta

1. Preheat oven to 375°F and coat a 13" × 9" baking dish with 1 tablespoon olive oil.

2. Place chicken breasts in baking dish and season with salt.

3. Cover chicken with chipotle and green pepper and onion slices and drizzle with 1 tablespoon olive oil. Bake for 25 minutes or until juices run clear.

4. Remove chicken from oven and stir in spinach until wilted.

5. Pour 1 cup polenta into each of two serving bowls and cover each with half of the chicken and peppers mixture; serve hot.

PER SERVING   Calories: 489 | Fat: 9.6 grams | Protein: 31.8 grams | Sodium: 884 milligrams | Fiber: 4.1 grams | Carbohydrates: 63.4 grams | Sugar: 2.7 grams

POWER SOURCES

CHICKEN: low in calories per ounce, but high in protein for natural energy support

BELL PEPPER: antioxidants safeguard cell health

POLENTA: adds natural carbohydrates for clean energy production

Summer Squash Soup with Greens and Cream

Prep Time: 10 minutes | **Cook Time:** 20 minutes | **Serves 2**

2 tablespoons coconut oil, divided

2 cups chopped kale

2 large acorn squash, peeled, seeded, and chopped into ½" cubes

1 tablespoon honey

2 cups unsweetened almond milk

1½ teaspoons ground nutmeg, divided

½ cup nonfat yogurt

1 Coat the bottom of a large pot with 1 tablespoon coconut oil and heat over medium heat.

2 Add kale and cook for 5 minutes or until softened; remove from pot and set aside.

3 Coat the large pot with the remaining 1 tablespoon coconut oil and heat over medium heat. Add squash and cook for 5 minutes, stirring constantly until squash is slightly softened.

4 Add honey and almond milk and bring to a simmer for 10–15 minutes or until squash is fork-tender.

5 Return kale to pot and sprinkle with 1 teaspoon nutmeg. Using an immersion blender, blend soup on high until all ingredients are emulsified.

6 Pour half of soup into each of two serving bowls. Top each bowl with ¼ cup yogurt and ¼ teaspoon nutmeg. Serve warm.

PER SERVING   Calories: 371 | Fat: 13.2 grams | Protein: 8.7 grams | Sodium: 226 milligrams | Fiber: 6.9 grams | Carbohydrates: 60.4 grams | Sugar: 13.6 grams

POWER SOURCES

ACORN SQUASH: beta carotene acts as an immunity-supporting antioxidant

YOGURT: calcium is used in the neuromuscular reactions required for movement

KALE: vitamin K and potassium are used in energy-promoting enzyme reactions

☀ POWER BOWL PRIORITIES

The idea of carb loading isn't a new concept to avid athletes who prepare their meals mindfully when prepping for competitions, races, or other athletic ambitions, but even the average Joe can benefit from nutrients found in natural carbohydrates. With whole grains, fresh fruits, and vibrant vegetables that provide the body and brain with essential complex carbohydrates, power bowls ensure that blood sugar levels remain consistent throughout the day and that the fuel required by the body for endurance and stamina is readily available. With fresh, whole foods like these, the entire body benefits.

Loaded Baked Potato Bowl

Prep Time: 10 minutes | **Cook Time:** 24 minutes | **Serves 2**

1 (12-ounce) package turkey bacon

½ small yellow onion, peeled and chopped

2 small russet potatoes, peeled and chopped into ¼" pieces

2 teaspoons olive oil

¼ cup water

2 cups spinach

½ cup Greek yogurt

4 tablespoons shredded Cheddar cheese

4 tablespoons chopped fresh chives

POWER SOURCES

POTATO: fiber regulates blood sugar for sustained energy

BACON: B vitamins increase output of energizing brain biochemicals

SPINACH: magnesium for muscle fiber strength

1 In a large skillet over medium heat, place 6 bacon strips and cook for 3–5 minutes per side or until cooked through; set aside. Repeat with remaining bacon slices.

2 Add onions and potatoes to skillet and drizzle with olive oil. Stir potatoes and onions every 2 minutes, adding 2 tablespoons of the water if necessary to prevent sticking or burning. Sauté until potatoes are fork-tender, about 10–12 minutes.

3 Remove skillet from heat and add spinach. Stir to combine well until spinach is wilted, about 2 minutes.

4 Add an equal amount of potato mixture to each of two serving bowls. Top each bowl with ¼ cup Greek yogurt, then crumble half of the cooked bacon over top of each bowl. Top each bowl's bacon with 2 tablespoons Cheddar cheese and 2 tablespoons chives. Serve warm.

PER SERVING   Calories: 621 | Fat: 36.7 grams | Protein: 38.6 grams | Sodium: 2193 milligrams | Fiber: 3.1 grams | Carbohydrates: 29.3 grams | Sugar: 4.1 grams

Chai Chia Pudding with Berries

Prep Time: 12–24 hours | **Cook Time:** N/A | **Serves 1**

1 cup blueberries, divided

1 tablespoon honey

1 cup Greek yogurt

1 cup vanilla almond milk

2 tablespoons ground flaxseed

1 cup chia seeds, divided

1 teaspoon cinnamon

1 teaspoon cardamom

1 tablespoon whole flaxseed

1 In a large glass bowl with a tight-fitting lid, crush ½ cup of the blueberries.

2 Add honey, Greek yogurt, and almond milk and whisk together until thoroughly combined.

3 Add ground flaxseed, ¾ cup chia seeds, cinnamon, and cardamom to the mixture and whisk to blend.

4 Cover and refrigerate for 12–24 hours or until set and thickened.

5 Uncover and top with remaining ½ cup blueberries, whole flaxseed, and ¼ cup chia seeds. Serve chilled.

PER SERVING   Calories: 1373 | Fat: 73.6 grams | Protein: 54.7 grams | Sodium: 273 milligrams | Fiber: 66.5 grams | Carbohydrates: 141.3 grams | Sugar: 57.3 grams

POWER SOURCES

CHIA SEEDS: filling fiber improves digestion and absorption of nutrients

GREEK YOGURT: calcium and magnesium improve reaction times

HONEY: natural sugars maintain sustained levels of energy

CINNAMON: rich antioxidants safeguard cells against oxidative damage

BLUEBERRIES: fiber prevents dips in energy levels

FLAXSEED: omega-3s support brain and muscle health

❋ POWER BOWL PRIORITIES

Cinnamon provides plentiful phytochemicals and compounds that stimulate the metabolism and act as potent antioxidants. The combination of these two elements not only cleanses the brain and bloodstream of energy-zapping toxins, but it also helps to prevent mental fogginess throughout the day.

Grilled Chicken Salad with Crunchy Quinoa

Prep Time: 5 minutes | **Cook Time:** N/A | **Serves 2**

2 (4-ounce) chicken breasts, grilled and cooled

2 teaspoons salt, divided

1 teaspoon black pepper

3 celery stalks, chopped

2 cups cooked quinoa

½ cup plus 4 tablespoons golden raisins, divided

1 cup Greek yogurt

1 tablespoon apple cider vinegar

1 teaspoon garlic powder

1 Chop or pull chicken into bite-sized pieces and place in a large bowl. Season with 1 teaspoon salt and pepper.

2 Add celery, quinoa, and ½ cup raisins to chicken and stir to combine thoroughly.

3 Stir in Greek yogurt and vinegar and toss to coat. Season with garlic powder and remaining 1 teaspoon salt.

4 Pour equal amounts of chicken salad into each of two serving bowls. Garnish each with 2 tablespoons golden raisins. Serve chilled.

PER SERVING   Calories: 632 | Fat: 10.9 grams | Protein: 45.1 grams | Sodium: 2432 milligrams | Fiber: 8.8 grams | Carbohydrates: 90.9 grams | Sugar: 39.2 grams

POWER SOURCES

CELERY: antioxidants and vitamins C and K combine to support immunity

YOGURT: calcium supports bone strength and blood health

CHICKEN: protein and B vitamins ensure optimal muscle and blood health

QUINOA: contains all essential amino acids for maximized muscle functioning and support

CHAPTER 3
Postworkout Recovery Bowls

The postworkout power bowls found in this chapter contain an assortment of foods that provide the entire body with a wide variety of nutrients that help restore and repair the muscles, tissues, and organ systems involved in exercise. Each of these bowls is packed with:

- Proteins that help repair your muscles and prepare your body to use carbohydrates for future energy use.
- Greens, fruits, and grains that supply rich amounts of natural sugars, sodium, potassium, calcium, B vitamins, vitamin C, and vitamin E. These nutrients combine to help support the functioning of your cardiovascular and immune systems and aid in digestion. Efficient digestion maximizes nutrient absorption into the bloodstream for optimal delivery of the essentials to all of the organs, muscles, and systems for postworkout repair.
- Fiber, like that found in the ingredients used in this chapter like chicken, lean beef, tofu, and vegetables and fruits, stabilizes blood sugar levels; supports the repair and replenishment of muscle, bone, and tissue cells; and supports the conversion of carbohydrates to energy for the next workout naturally and deliciously!

In addition, these delicious bowls combine vibrantly colored produce with flavorful spices and grains to enhance your metabolism and minimize inflammation. These ingredients not only support your body's previous workout results with plentiful provisions of carbohydrates, protein, vitamins, and minerals, but also prepare it for the next workout, too! With creamy additions and filling fiber, each and every recipe is designed to deliver quality nutrition for amazing results.

Fried Eggs over Dirty Rice with Salsa and Avocado

Prep Time: 10 minutes | **Cook Time:** 8 minutes | **Serves 2**

1 tablespoon olive oil

4 large eggs

2 large tomatoes, chopped

½ cup peeled and chopped sweet onion

¼ cup chopped fresh cilantro

½ lime, juiced

½ teaspoon salt

1 teaspoon garlic powder

2 cups prepared brown rice

1 cup canned, rinsed, and drained black beans

½ teaspoon cayenne

1 small avocado, peeled, pitted, and sliced

1. Coat a large skillet with olive oil and heat over medium-high heat.

2. Break eggs into skillet and cook for 3–4 minutes, turn, and cook for an additional 3–4 minutes until whites are cooked and yolks are cooked to desired consistency. Remove from heat.

3. In a small bowl, combine chopped tomatoes, onion, cilantro, lime juice, ½ teaspoon salt, and garlic powder, and toss to combine. Set aside.

4. In a large bowl, combine prepared rice, black beans, and cayenne.

5. Pour equal amounts of rice mixture into each of two serving bowls. Top each bowl's rice with 2 fried eggs, equal amounts of tomato salsa, and half the avocado slices. Serve warm.

PER SERVING   Calories: 649 | Fat: 23.0 grams | Protein: 28.7 grams | Sodium: 897 milligrams | Fiber: 18.8 grams | Carbohydrates: 79.8 grams | Sugar: 6.7 grams

POWER SOURCES

EGG: choline supports brain health for optimized system functioning

BROWN RICE: soluble fiber supports mineral absorption for improved muscle-related processes

BLACK BEANS: protein maintains muscle mass

AVOCADO: healthy monounsaturated fats support brain, blood, and muscle health

Banana Nut Chia Pudding

Prep Time: 12–24 hours | **Cook Time:** N/A | **Serves 1**

1 medium banana, peeled and
  sliced

2 cups vanilla almond milk

1 teaspoon maple syrup

1 teaspoon cinnamon

½ cup shelled walnuts

½ cup chia seeds

POWER SOURCES

BANANA: potassium supports
the recovery and replenishment
of nutrients in muscles

WALNUTS: antioxidants
support healthy metabolic
functions of cells

CHIA SEEDS: fiber supports
stable blood sugar levels for
optimal repair and preparation
in muscles

1 In a blender, combine the banana and almond milk and
   blend on high until well blended, about 1 minute.

2 Add maple syrup, cinnamon, and walnuts to the
   blender and blend on high until walnuts are emulsified,
   about 1–2 minutes.

3 Pour contents of blender into a bowl with a tight-fitting
   lid and stir in chia seeds until thoroughly combined.

4 Cover and refrigerate for 12–24 hours until desired
   consistency is achieved. Serve cold.

PER SERVING   Calories: 1023 | Fat: 61.2 grams | Protein:
24.6 grams | Sodium: 334 milligrams | Fiber:
35.0 grams | Carbohydrates: 105.9 grams | Sugar: 51.8 grams

☀ POWER BOWL PRIORITIES

Whether making a coffee, smoothie, or a dessert,
you're going to need some sort of sweetening agent.
However, you can opt to use natural alternatives to
harmful products such as high-fructose corn syrup.
Many of the recipes throughout the book use organic
honey or maple syrup to provide extra sweetness. These
natural ingredients provide essential vitamins, minerals,
phytochemicals, and phytonutrients that can actually act
to promote health while combatting microbes, bacteria,
fungi, and viruses.

Rice Noodles with Creamy Citrus Chicken and Greens

Prep Time: 10 minutes | **Cook Time:** 15 minutes | **Serves 2**

1 tablespoon olive oil

1 cup chopped kale leaves

1 teaspoon garlic powder

1 teaspoon salt

1 (4-ounce) chicken breast, cut into ½" cubes

¼ cup lemon juice

1 tablespoon honey

¼ cup Greek yogurt

2 cups prepared rice noodles

1. Coat a large skillet with olive oil and heat over medium heat. Add kale leaves to the skillet and sprinkle them with garlic powder and salt. Then sauté until wilted, about 5 minutes.

2. Add chicken, lemon juice, and honey to skillet and sauté until chicken is cooked through, about 5–7 minutes.

3. Slowly add Greek yogurt and stir to distribute evenly.

4. Pour 1 cup rice noodles into each of two serving bowls and top each bowl with half the chicken-kale mixture. Serve warm.

PER SERVING   Calories: 368 | Fat: 7.3 grams | Protein: 18.5 grams | Sodium: 1209 milligrams | Fiber: 2.3 grams | Carbohydrates: 55.8 grams | Sugar: 10.7 grams

POWER SOURCES

GREEK YOGURT: calcium and potassium support muscle functioning

CHICKEN: B vitamins repair muscles postworkout

LEMON: limonins act to safeguard tissues against damage by free radicals

Citrus-Mango Tofu with Asparagus and Brown Rice

Prep Time: 15 minutes | **Cook Time:** 20 minutes | **Serves 2**

½ cup water

2 cups asparagus spears

1 teaspoon salt

1 garlic clove, minced

1 tablespoon olive oil

8 ounces extra-firm tofu, cut into ½" cubes

½ cup grapefruit juice

1 cup peeled and sliced mango

2 cups prepared brown rice

½ lemon, seeded and sliced

1 In a large skillet over medium-high heat, combine water and asparagus. Sprinkle with salt and add minced garlic. Cover and steam for 5 minutes or until spears are fork-tender. Remove from skillet and set aside.

2 Drizzle olive oil in skillet and add tofu. Sauté tofu over medium heat for 7–10 minutes or until slightly golden brown.

3 Add grapefruit juice to tofu while stirring, then sauté for 5 minutes or until juice thickens. Add mango slices to skillet and stir to thoroughly combine. Remove from heat.

4 Layer 1 cup brown rice, half the asparagus spears, and half the tofu mixture in each of two serving bowls. Garnish each bowl with half the lemon slices. Serve warm.

PER SERVING   Calories: 442 | Fat: 11.2 grams | Protein: 17.9 grams | Sodium: 1181 milligrams | Fiber: 8.8 grams | Carbohydrates: 71.4 grams | Sugar: 20.0 grams

POWER SOURCES

GRAPEFRUIT: vitamin C promotes a healthy immune system

MANGO: beta carotene improves brain functions related to healing hormone production

BROWN RICE: fiber promotes satiety during and after workouts

Crispy Tempeh with Spicy Slaw and Yogurt Dressing

Prep Time: 15 minutes | **Cook Time:** 10 minutes | **Serves 2**

1 large egg

1 teaspoon salt

1 teaspoon garlic powder

½ cup panko bread crumbs

2 tablespoons olive oil

4 ounces tempeh, cut into ¼"-thick sections

1 teaspoon honey

½ cup peeled and matchstick-sized-sliced carrots

½ cup matchstick-sized-sliced purple cabbage

1 teaspoon grated ginger

½ cup nonfat yogurt

¼ teaspoon cayenne

1. Add egg, salt, and garlic powder to a large bowl and whisk to combine. Then add panko to a large plate.

2. Coat a large skillet with olive oil and heat over medium-high heat. Dredge the tempeh into the egg mixture, coat with panko, and place into large skillet and sauté until slightly browned, about 3–5 minutes. Flip and cook until browned, about 3–5 minutes. Repeat for remaining tempeh.

3. Drizzle tempeh with honey and set aside.

4. In a large bowl, combine carrots, cabbage, ginger, yogurt, and cayenne and toss to thoroughly combine.

5. Pour half the slaw into each of two serving bowls. Place half the tempeh on top of each bowl. Serve warm or chilled.

PER SERVING Calories: 388 | Fat: 20.6 grams | Protein: 19.4 grams | Sodium: 1316 milligrams | Fiber: 1.7 grams | Carbohydrates: 22.8 grams | Sugar: 9.9 grams

POWER SOURCES

TEMPEH: soy provides the body with complete protein

CABBAGE: antioxidants protect the body from free-radical damage

YOGURT: calcium regulates sleep and wake cycles for better energy and repair

Creamy Chicken, Black Beans, and Quinoa

Prep Time: 10 minutes | **Cook Time:** 25 minutes | **Serves 2**

2 tablespoons olive oil, divided

1 (4-ounce) chicken breast

1 small yellow onion, peeled and chopped

1 teaspoon salt

1 teaspoon garlic powder

½ teaspoon cayenne

1 cup chopped tomatoes

2 tablespoons lime juice

½ cup canned, rinsed, and drained black beans

2 cups prepared quinoa

2 whole-wheat tortillas, cut into ¼" strips

1 cup nonfat yogurt

½ cup chopped fresh cilantro

1 Coat a large skillet with 1 tablespoon olive oil and heat over medium heat. Add chicken breast and cook for 5–7 minutes on each side or until golden brown. Remove from heat, cool, and shred.

2 Coat skillet with 1 tablespoon olive oil, add onions, and sauté 5–7 minutes over medium heat until onions are translucent.

3 Add salt, garlic powder, cayenne, tomatoes, lime juice, black beans, chicken, and quinoa. Stir to combine thoroughly and heat through, about 2 minutes. Remove from heat and cool for 5 minutes.

4 Place half the tortilla strips in each of two serving bowls. Toss chicken mixture with yogurt and layer equal amounts of mixture on tortilla strips in each bowl.

5 Garnish each bowl with ¼ cup cilantro and serve hot.

PER SERVING   Calories: 503 | Fat: 13.1 grams | Protein: 37.1 grams | Sodium: 1685 milligrams | Fiber: 14.5 grams | Carbohydrates: 93.5 grams | Sugar: 18.1 grams

POWER SOURCES

TOMATO: vitamin A acts as an antioxidant to combat free radicals

CILANTRO: phytochemicals support cellular health

QUINOA: amino acids repair damage to muscles from physical activity

❋ POWER BOWL PRIORITIES

To maximize the nutritional benefits in each power bowl, consider future activities before planning what to put in your dish. If you're going to be working out or doing strenuous activities that require energy, focus on complex carbs and healthy fats. If you're going to be recovering from a workout, resting and relaxing, or heading to bed, keep the carbs lighter and focus more on protein and hydration. By pairing your power bowls with your activities, you can boost your benefits with every delicious and nutritious meal.

Beet Salad with Honey-Ginger Tofu

Prep Time: 5 minutes | **Cook Time:** 5 minutes | **Serves 2**

2 tablespoons olive oil, divided

8 ounces extra-firm tofu, sliced into ½" strips

1" gingerroot, peeled and sliced thin

2 tablespoons honey

4 cups spinach

1 cup prepared millet

2 small cooked beets, peeled and thinly sliced (preferably with a mandoline)

1 Coat a large skillet with 1 tablespoon olive oil and heat over medium heat. Add tofu and ginger. Drizzle ingredients with honey and sauté for 5 minutes or until tofu is slightly browned. Remove from heat to cool.

2 Add 2 cups fresh spinach to each of two serving bowls. Top each bowl with ½ cup millet and an equal amount of beets.

3 Pour half of the tofu mixture into each bowl and drizzle each bowl with ½ tablespoon olive oil.

PER SERVING   Calories: 654 | Fat: 19.8 grams | Protein: 24.9 grams | Sodium: 99 milligrams | Fiber: 11.3 grams | Carbohydrates: 95.2 grams | Sugar: 17.6 grams

POWER SOURCES

TOFU: soy protein regenerates muscle tissue

BEETS: betalain promotes detoxifying processes in the liver

SPINACH: iron acts to promote oxygen delivery to muscles

Spicy Beef with Fiery Fresh Vegetables and Barley

Prep Time: 10 minutes | **Cook Time:** 12 minutes | **Serves 2**

2 tablespoons olive oil

1 small yellow onion, peeled and sliced

1 cup peeled and thinly sliced carrots

¼ cup water

12 ounces London broil, sliced thin

1 large zucchini, sliced

1 teaspoon salt

1 teaspoon minced garlic

½ teaspoon cayenne

2 cups prepared barley

1 Coat a large skillet with olive oil and heat over medium heat. Add onions and carrots. Sauté for 1 minute, then add water to slightly steam until fork-tender, about 5 minutes.

2 Add steak and sauté about 3 minutes or until slightly pink.

3 Add zucchini, salt, garlic, and cayenne and sauté until zucchini is slightly fork-tender, about 3 minutes. Remove from heat.

4 Pour 1 cup barley into each of two serving bowls and top each with equal amounts of steak mixture. Serve hot.

PER SERVING   Calories: 536 | Fat: 13.5 grams | Protein: 46.4 grams | Sodium: 1318 milligrams | Fiber: 9.9 grams | Carbohydrates: 58.6 grams | Sugar: 8.6 grams

POWER SOURCES

LONDON BROIL: B vitamins help essential hormones function more efficiently

CARROT: beta carotene can help reduce exercise-induced asthma

ZUCCHINI: water content and minerals combine for essential hydration of cells

Vegetarian Lasagna with Roasted Vegetables

Prep Time: 15 minutes | **Cook Time:** 30 minutes | **Serves 2**

4 cups water

4 brown rice lasagna noodles

2 tablespoons olive oil, divided

1 medium eggplant, sliced into
   ¼"-thick rounds

3 small tomatoes, sliced into
   ½"-thick rounds

1 large zucchini, sliced into
   ¼"-thick rounds

1 teaspoon salt

1 teaspoon garlic powder

4 kale leaves, chopped

1 cup shredded mozzarella cheese

1 Pour water into a large pot over high heat and bring to a boil. Break lasagna noodles in half to make 8 equal-sized noodles. Add noodles to water.

2 Preheat oven to 400°F and grease a large baking sheet with 1 tablespoon olive oil. Layer eggplant, tomatoes, and zucchini on baking sheet, sprinkle with salt and garlic powder, and bake for 5 minutes. Turn and bake an additional 5–7 minutes or until fork-tender. Remove from heat.

3 While vegetables are baking, cook pasta until al dente, about 7–10 minutes. Remove pasta from water and add kale to water. Cook for 5 minutes and remove from heat. Remove kale from water and drain.

4 Layer in each of two serving bowls 1 lasagna noodle; a quarter of each serving of eggplant, zucchini, tomato, and kale; and ¼ cup mozzarella.

5 Repeat layering process three more times for each bowl and serve hot.

PER SERVING   Calories: 541 | Fat: 21.9 grams | Protein: 23.6 grams | Sodium: 1573 milligrams | Fiber: 11.2 grams | Carbohydrates: 64.2 grams | Sugar: 16.5 grams

POWER SOURCES

EGGPLANT: essential minerals promote energy-production processes for rapid recovery

TOMATO: vitamin A acts as an antioxidant to combat free radicals

KALE: vitamin D aids in retainment of muscle and bone tissue health

Pesto-Tossed Salmon with Tomato-Spinach Quinoa

Prep Time: 10 minutes | **Cook Time:** 15 minutes | **Serves 2**

2 tablespoons plus ½ cup olive oil, divided

2 (4-ounce) salmon fillets

½ cup fresh basil

3 garlic cloves

¼ cup shredded Parmesan cheese

2 cups cooked quinoa

1 cup halved cherry tomatoes

1 cup chopped spinach

1 tablespoon balsamic vinegar

POWER SOURCES

OLIVE OIL: monounsaturated fats support healthy cholesterol levels in the blood

BASIL: phytonutrients prevent the oxidation of muscle and cardiovascular cells

SALMON: zinc promotes healthy muscle contraction to help reduce cramping postworkout

1 Preheat oven to 375°F and coat a 9" × 9" pan with 1 tablespoon olive oil. Place fish fillets in pan and cook for 15 minutes or until fish is flaky and cooked through. Remove from heat and set aside.

2 In a blender, combine ½ cup olive oil, basil, garlic, and Parmesan and blend on high until emulsified. Set aside.

3 In a large mixing bowl, combine quinoa, cherry tomatoes, spinach, remaining 1 tablespoon olive oil, and balsamic vinegar and toss to thoroughly combine. Pour equal amounts of quinoa mixture into each of two serving bowls.

4 In the same large mixing bowl, shred salmon and pour pesto over top. Toss to coat salmon chunks thoroughly.

5 Layer half the pesto-coated salmon in each serving bowl and serve cool.

PER SERVING   Calories: 1004 | Fat: 72.0 grams | Protein: 36.8 grams | Sodium: 285 milligrams | Fiber: 6.6 grams | Carbohydrates: 46.2 grams | Sugar: 5.0 grams

Blueberry Muffin Smoothie Bowl

Prep Time: 5 minutes | **Cook Time:** N/A | **Serves 2**

1 medium banana, peeled and
   sliced

2 cups blueberries plus
   2 teaspoons, divided

1 cup cooked rolled oats

½ tablespoon cinnamon

3 cups almond milk

2 cups ice

1. In a large blender, combine banana, 2 cups blueberries, oats, cinnamon, and almond milk and blend on high until thoroughly combined and emulsified.

2. Add ice gradually while blending on high and blend until smooth.

3. Pour half the smoothie mixture into each of two serving bowls. Top each bowl with 1 teaspoon blueberries. Serve cold.

PER SERVING Calories: 315 | Fat: 5.7 grams | Protein: 6.3 grams | Sodium: 246 milligrams | Fiber: 8.2 grams | Carbohydrates: 63.0 grams | Sugar: 33.1 grams

POWER SOURCES

BANANA: potassium aids in muscle contraction and repair

OATS: fiber regulates insulin levels for sustained energy postworkout

CINNAMON: antioxidants prevent oxidative effects on cells within muscles and bones

CHAPTER 4
Bowls for Weight Loss

Anyone who has struggled with weight loss knows all too well that diet and exercise play intricate roles in achieving and maintaining the success of desired weight goals. With smoothies, salads, and entrées that help placate hunger while satisfying your body's needs for nutrients, each and every power bowl recipe in this chapter is packed with a combination of proteins, complex carbohydrates, fats, and supplemental vitamins and minerals. These nutrients are needed to help fuel your body's energy, endurance, and ability to repair itself, ensuring that an optimal balance is maintained at all times for all systems.

With foods, spices, and creamy additions that fulfill the body's nutritional needs, support the body's natural systems' functioning, and satisfy cravings of all kinds, these power bowl recipes will help you achieve optimal health—and your weight-loss goals!

Ginger-Snap Smoothie Bowl

Prep Time: 5 minutes | **Cook Time:** N/A | **Serves 2**

1" gingerroot, peeled

2 cups almond milk

½ cup shelled walnuts

¼ cup ground flaxseed

2 teaspoons cinnamon, divided

1 tablespoon maple syrup

1 cup ice

POWER SOURCES

GINGER: gingerol and shogaol may prevent inflammation

WALNUTS: phytonutrients may help reduce the risk of developing some cancers

ALMOND MILK: calcium helps promote healthy bones if fortified almond milk is used

FLAXSEED: promotes healthy cholesterol levels in the blood

1 In a large blender, combine ginger, almond milk, and walnuts and blend on high until ginger and walnuts are emulsified, about 1–2 minutes.

2 Add flaxseed, 1 teaspoon cinnamon, and maple syrup to blender and blend on high until all ingredients are thoroughly combined, about 1 minute.

3 Add ice gradually while blending on high and blend until smooth.

4 Pour equal amounts of smoothie into each of two serving bowls and garnish each bowl with ½ teaspoon cinnamon. Serve cold.

PER SERVING   Calories: 330 | Fat: 24.1 grams | Protein: 6.9 grams | Sodium: 165 milligrams | Fiber: 7.1 grams | Carbohydrates: 24.4 grams | Sugar: 13.8 grams

Shrimp Scampi with Rice Noodles

Prep Time: 10 minutes | **Cook Time:** 15 minutes | **Serves 2**

4 cups water

1 (8-ounce) package rice noodles

1 tablespoon olive oil

1 small yellow onion, peeled and chopped

1 pound shrimp, peeled and deveined

1 garlic clove, minced

1 teaspoon salt

¼ cup lemon juice, divided

1 large tomato, chopped

½ cup fresh basil

¼ teaspoon cayenne

1. In a large pot, bring water to a boil. Add rice noodles and cook until al dente, about 3 minutes. Remove from heat and strain.

2. Coat a large skillet with olive oil and heat over medium heat. Add onions and sauté until translucent, about 5 minutes.

3. Add shrimp, garlic, salt, and ⅛ cup lemon juice and sauté until shrimp are cooked through, about 5 minutes.

4. Add tomatoes, basil, rice noodles, cayenne, and remaining ⅛ cup lemon juice and stir to combine and heat through, about 2 minutes.

5. Pour equal amounts of the scampi into each of two serving bowls and serve hot.

PER SERVING   Calories: 687 | Fat: 6.4 grams | Protein: 53.9 grams | Sodium: 1643 milligrams | Fiber: 3.7 grams | Carbohydrates: 100.3 grams | Sugar: 4.7 grams

POWER SOURCES

SHRIMP: zinc improves blood oxygen levels

OLIVE OIL: healthy fats reduce LDL cholesterol

BASIL: phytonutrients protect cells against free-radical damage

✳ POWER BOWL PRIORITIES

If you're serious about reaping the benefits from these hardworking power bowls, you want to put that cocktail aside. Alcohol directly and adversely affects the nutritional benefits of these potent power bowls by providing sugars, carbohydrates, and hard-to-digest alcohols that make natural detoxification more difficult. By limiting alcohol consumption, the liver, kidneys, digestive system, brain and nervous system, and cardiovascular system all maintain focus on their primary responsibilities rather than alcohol processing and detoxification.

Cool Cobb Salad Bowl

Prep Time: 5 minutes | **Cook Time:** N/A | **Serves 2**

4 cups chopped romaine lettuce

2 tablespoons olive oil

1 tablespoon apple cider vinegar

2 large hard-boiled eggs, sliced

1 (4-ounce) grilled and shredded chicken breast

1 small avocado, peeled, pitted, and sliced

2 large tomatoes, chopped

1 medium cucumber, peeled and chopped

1 In a large bowl combine romaine lettuce, olive oil, and vinegar and toss to coat.

2 Pour even amounts of salad mixture into each of two serving bowls and top each with half the egg slices, chicken, avocado, tomato, and cucumber. Serve cold.

PER SERVING Calories: 431 | Fat: 28.0 grams | Protein: 23.0 grams | Sodium: 85 milligrams | Fiber: 9.5 grams | Carbohydrates: 18.9 grams | Sugar: 8.1 grams

POWER SOURCES

ROMAINE LETTUCE: vitamin C promotes immune system functioning

CHICKEN: B vitamins strengthen bones and muscles

AVOCADO: potassium promotes muscle cell functioning

Caprese Tofu-Stuffed Tomatoes

Prep Time: 5 minutes | **Cook Time:** 10 minutes | **Serves 2**

2 tablespoons olive oil

8 ounces extra-firm tofu, crumbled

1 teaspoon salt

1 teaspoon garlic powder

2 large beefsteak tomatoes

½ cup chopped fresh basil, divided

¼ cup balsamic vinegar

1 cup cooked quinoa

½ cup shredded mozzarella cheese

POWER SOURCES

TOMATO: lycopene acts as a potent antioxidant for cell health protection

GARLIC: sulfur compounds may decrease the production of cholesterol in the liver

QUINOA: fiber aids in the healthy functioning of the liver's bile production processes

1 Coat a large skillet with olive oil and heat over medium heat. Add tofu, then sprinkle with salt and garlic powder and sauté until crumbles are cooked and slightly browned, about 7–10 minutes.

2 Slice the tops off of the large beefsteak tomatoes and scrape insides into skillet with tofu, keeping the tomato skins intact to act as a bowl.

3 Add ¼ cup basil, vinegar, and quinoa to skillet and stir to heat through.

4 Place 1 hollowed tomato in each of two serving bowls, pour equal amounts of tofu mixture into each, and top each with ¼ cup mozzarella and ⅛ cup basil. Serve hot or cold.

PER SERVING   Calories: 455 | Fat: 22.9 grams | Protein: 24.4 grams | Sodium: 1386 milligrams | Fiber: 5.5 grams | Carbohydrates: 37.6 grams | Sugar: 11.6 grams

Sautéed Vegetables and Penne with Spicy Marinara

Prep Time: 10 minutes | **Cook Time:** 45 minutes | **Serves 2**

1 cup water

4 small tomatoes (2 chopped, 2 crushed)

1 teaspoon salt

¼ teaspoon cayenne

1 tablespoon olive oil

1 small yellow onion, peeled and chopped

½ small zucchini, sliced

½ small yellow squash, sliced

2 cloves garlic, minced

2 cups cooked whole-wheat penne pasta

1 In a pot over medium heat, heat water. Add the chopped and crushed tomatoes to the water. Season with salt and cayenne, bring to a boil, and reduce heat to simmer. Simmer for 20–25 minutes or until thickened.

2 Coat a large skillet with olive oil and heat over medium heat. Add onions. Sauté until onions are tender, about 5 minutes.

3 Add zucchini, squash, and garlic to skillet and sauté for 5–7 minutes or until squash are fork-tender.

4 Add cooked penne to marinara and stir until heated through. Remove from heat.

5 Pour equal amounts of penne and sauce into each of two serving bowls and top each with equal amounts of onions, zucchini, and squash. Serve hot.

PER SERVING   Calories: 282 | Fat: 7.3 grams | Protein: 10.9 grams | Sodium: 1182 milligrams | Fiber: 9.4 grams | Carbohydrates: 52.0 grams | Sugar: 7.5 grams

POWER SOURCES

ZUCCHINI: sodium supports nervous system functions related to the heart

ONION: allicin provides antimicrobial benefits to fight common germs and improve immunity

TOMATO: lycopene acts as an antioxidant for cell health protection

WHOLE-WHEAT PENNE: fiber helps promote satiety and can reduce overeating by keeping the body feeling full for longer periods of time

Sweet Beets and Berries in Yogurt with Oats

Prep Time: 10 minutes | **Cook Time:** 20 minutes | **Serves 2**

¼ cup water

2 small beets

1 tablespoon lemon juice

1 tablespoon honey

1 cup Greek yogurt

1 cup cooked rolled oats

1 cup blueberries

1 teaspoon ground cinnamon

POWER SOURCES

BEETS: betalain protects and repairs liver cells required for metabolism

BLUEBERRIES: flavonoids support cellular structure and promote immune system functioning

YOGURT: probiotics provide healthy bacteria for optimal immune system functioning

1 Preheat oven to 400°F and prepare a 9" × 9" pan with ¼ cup water. Remove tops from beets and place beets in pan. Bake beets for 20 minutes or until fork-tender, remove from heat, remove skins, and slice to a ¼" thickness.

2 In a large bowl, combine beets and lemon juice. Toss to coat.

3 Drizzle with honey and add yogurt. Toss to combine and thoroughly coat.

4 Place ½ cup oats into each of two serving bowls, then top each with half the beet mixture.

5 Top each bowl with ½ cup blueberries and ½ teaspoon cinnamon; serve cold.

PER SERVING   Calories: 359 | Fat: 8.9 grams | Protein: 16.8 grams | Sodium: 79 milligrams | Fiber: 7.5 grams | Carbohydrates: 57.4 grams | Sugar: 25.6 grams

Curried Chicken Salad Bowl

Prep Time: 5 minutes | **Cook Time:** N/A | **Serves 2**

1 cup nonfat Greek yogurt

1 tablespoon apple cider vinegar

1 teaspoon ground turmeric

1 teaspoon curry powder

1 teaspoon honey

1 (4-ounce) grilled and shredded chicken breast

1 large tomato, chopped

1 cup cooked quinoa

4 cups chopped romaine lettuce

½ cup peeled and minced red onion

1 In a large bowl, combine yogurt, vinegar, turmeric, curry, and honey and whisk until thoroughly combined.

2 Add chicken, tomato, and quinoa to bowl and toss to thoroughly combine.

3 Add romaine to bowl and toss to coat evenly.

4 Pour equal amounts of chicken salad into each of two serving bowls and top each with ¼ cup onion. Serve chilled.

PER SERVING   Calories: 293 | Fat: 2.9 grams | Protein: 30.1 grams | Sodium: 66 milligrams | Fiber: 6.8 grams | Carbohydrates: 36.8 grams | Sugar: 12.4 grams

POWER SOURCES

CHICKEN: B vitamins support and sustain energy production

ROMAINE LETTUCE: vitamin K supports antioxidant activity in the cells and tissues

YOGURT: calcium supports energy and balances mood

QUINOA: fiber helps promote satiety and can reduce overeating by keeping the body feeling full for longer periods of time

Lemon Tempeh with Zucchini Pasta in Sweet Honey Yogurt

Prep Time: 15 minutes | **Cook Time:** 13 minutes | **Serves 2**

1 cup nonfat yogurt

1 tablespoon honey

2 large zucchini

1 tablespoon olive oil

8 ounces tempeh

1 teaspoon salt

2 tablespoons lemon juice

POWER SOURCES

ZUCCHINI: high water content hydrates the body

HONEY: natural sugars assist in curbing sugar cravings

YOGURT: calcium supports bone health

1 In a large bowl, whisk yogurt and honey to combine.

2 Using a spiralizer, create noodles from zucchini and place in bowl with yogurt mixture.

3 Coat a large skillet with olive oil and heat over medium heat. Add tempeh and cook for 3–5 minutes on each side until slightly browned.

4 Season tempeh with salt, then add lemon juice to skillet and cook tempeh for 2–3 minutes or until slightly golden. Remove from heat.

5 Place equal amounts of zucchini noodles in each of two serving bowls and top with equal amounts of tempeh. Serve warm or chilled.

PER SERVING   Calories: 433 | Fat: 17.6 grams | Protein: 31.9 grams | Sodium: 1291 milligrams | Fiber: 3.1 grams | Carbohydrates: 39.2 grams | Sugar: 26.0 grams

Watermelon-Kiwi Spinach Salad with Walnuts

Prep Time: 5 minutes | **Cook Time:** N/A | **Serves 2**

2 cups chopped (¼" chunks) and seeded watermelon

2 kiwis, peeled and sliced

4 cups spinach

1 cup prepared quinoa

1 tablespoon olive oil

1 tablespoon red wine vinegar

½ cup chopped shelled walnuts

¼ cup reduced-fat feta cheese

1 In a large bowl, combine watermelon and kiwi and stir to combine thoroughly.

2 Add spinach and stir to combine.

3 Add quinoa and toss to thoroughly combine.

4 Drizzle salad with oil and vinegar and toss to coat.

5 Pour equal amounts of the salad into each of two serving bowls and top each with ¼ cup walnuts and ⅛ cup feta. Serve chilled.

PER SERVING Calories: 470 | Fat: 26.5 grams | Protein: 14.9 grams | Sodium: 267 milligrams | Fiber: 8.5 grams | Carbohydrates: 48.4 grams | Sugar: 17.9 grams

POWER SOURCES

WATERMELON: high water content contributes to meeting daily fluid needs

KIWI: vitamin C promotes antioxidant benefits in muscles

SPINACH: folate supports healthy brain functioning

Tuna Niçoise Salad

Prep Time: 10 minutes | **Cook Time:** 5 minutes | **Serves 2**

4 tablespoons olive oil, divided

1 tablespoon Dijon mustard

4 cups chopped romaine lettuce

2 large hard-boiled eggs, halved lengthwise

1 cup halved cherry tomatoes

½ cup cooked French-cut green beans

2 (6-ounce) tuna steaks

1 teaspoon salt

1 teaspoon pepper

1 In a large bowl, whisk together 3 tablespoons olive oil and the Dijon mustard until thoroughly combined.

2 Add lettuce, eggs, tomatoes, and green beans to the bowl and toss to coat with the Dijon dressing.

3 Coat a large skillet with remaining 1 tablespoon olive oil and heat over medium-high heat. Season tuna steaks with salt and pepper and add to skillet. Cook steaks for 2 minutes per side for pink center and 3 minutes per side for opaque centers. Remove from heat and slice lengthwise, against the grain.

4 Pour equal amounts of tossed salad into each of two serving bowls and top each with 1 sliced tuna steak. Serve warm or chilled.

PER SERVING Calories: 621 | Fat: 35.2 grams | Protein: 51.0 grams | Sodium: 1349 milligrams | Fiber: 7.3 grams | Carbohydrates: 17.9 grams | Sugar: 3.7 grams

POWER SOURCES

GREEN BEANS: insoluble fiber cleanses the colon for improved digestion

EGG: methionine promotes healthy liver functioning to maximize metabolic functioning

TOMATO: vitamin C aids in the processes related to sustained energy production

✳ POWER BOWL PRIORITIES

Contrary to fad diets that promote limiting fats of all kind, these power bowls include healthy mono- and polyunsaturated fats that can be found in fish, flaxseed, nuts, and healthy oils. These fats are very beneficial to the body and brain, and can help you lose weight, raise your energy levels, help you age well, and keep your brain strong. They also contain rich provisions of health-boosting essential fats that help the heart, immune system, blood quality, and muscle functioning.

Chicken, Spinach, and Potatoes with Feta

Prep Time: 10 minutes | **Cook Time:** 35 minutes | **Serves 2**

2 tablespoons olive oil, divided

1 large Idaho potato, chopped into ¼" chunks

1 garlic clove, minced

2 (4-ounce) chicken breasts, cut into ½" strips

2 cups cherry tomatoes

1 teaspoon salt

1 teaspoon black pepper

1 teaspoon garlic powder

3 cups spinach

2 cups cooked jasmine rice

½ cup reduced-fat feta cheese

1 tablespoon chopped fresh basil

1 Preheat oven to 400°F and grease a 13" × 9" glass pan with 1 tablespoon olive oil. Scatter chopped potatoes and minced garlic in an even layer in the greased pan and roast for 10 minutes or until potatoes are slightly tender. Reduce heat to 375°F.

2 Layer chicken breasts on top of the potatoes in the pan and surround the chicken with the tomatoes. Drizzle with the remaining 1 tablespoon olive oil and sprinkle with salt, pepper, and garlic powder.

3 Bake for 15–20 minutes or until chicken's juices run clear.

4 Remove from heat and add spinach, rice, and feta to the pan. Fold all ingredients together in the pan and return to bake 5 minutes or until spinach is wilted and mixture is heated through.

5 Pour equal amounts of chicken mixture into each of two serving bowls. Garnish each with ½ tablespoon basil. Serve hot.

PER SERVING Calories: 617 | Fat: 12.9 grams | Protein: 41.5 grams | Sodium: 1656 milligrams | Fiber: 8.3 grams | Carbohydrates: 84.3 grams | Sugar: 6.4 grams

POWER SOURCES

TOMATO: carotenoids combat free-radical damage to cells

CHICKEN: choline supports processes related to fat metabolism

OLIVE OIL: omega-3s and omega-6s support blood health by reducing cholesterol and triglyceride levels

POTATO: digestion-resistant starches promote unhealthy brown-fat metabolism

CHAPTER 5

Bowls for Cleanses and Detox

Is your brain feeling foggy? Is your waistline bloated? Does your digestive system need support? Fortunately, the recipes in this chapter are packed full of cleansing ingredients that can help provide relief.

Typically, nutrients like potassium, calcium, and iron, as well as B vitamins and vitamins C, A, and E, can get left out of the standard American diet (appropriately termed SAD), which leaves the body's metabolic functioning and mental and cognitive abilities sluggish. But when you eat a diet packed with power bowls that cleanse and detoxify the body and brain of impurities, you'll find yourself enjoying whole foods that replenish cells; support your digestive, nervous, and cardiovascular systems; and maintain metabolic functioning. Delicious and nutritious, the power bowl recipes that you'll find here include a variety of proteins, fruits, vegetables, grains, and additions that make every meal and snack a satisfying step toward cleaner living.

Citrus Chicken with Cucumber-Tomato Quinoa

Prep Time: 10 minutes | **Cook Time:** 7 minutes | **Serves 2**

1 tablespoon olive oil

1 (4-ounce) chicken breast, cut into ¼" strips

2 tablespoons orange juice

2 tablespoons chopped rosemary

1 small cucumber, peeled and chopped

1 cup halved grape tomatoes

1 cup cooked quinoa

1 teaspoon salt

1 teaspoon pepper

1 Coat a large skillet with olive oil and heat over medium-high heat. Add chicken and orange juice and sauté for 5–7 minutes or until chicken is cooked through and juices run clear. Stir rosemary into chicken mixture and immediately remove from heat.

2 In a large bowl, toss together cucumber, tomatoes, and quinoa. Season with salt and pepper.

3 Layer equal amounts of quinoa mixture into each of two serving bowls and top each with equal amounts of citrus chicken mixture. Serve warm.

PER SERVING   Calories: 258 | Fat: 7.9 grams | Protein: 17.7 grams | Sodium: 1175 milligrams | Fiber: 5.9 grams | Carbohydrates: 28.8 grams | Sugar: 5.1 grams

POWER SOURCES

ORANGE JUICE: vitamin C helps improve immunity

CHICKEN: vitamin B_{12} supports healthy red blood cell production and repair

CUCUMBER: fiber helps remove waste and toxins from the body

TOMATO: bioflavonoids act to combat free-radical damage

Sweet Beet-Berry-Kiwi

Prep Time: 5 minutes | **Cook Time:** N/A | **Serves 2**

2 small red beets, roasted, peeled, and chopped

1 cup chopped pineapple

2 kiwis, peeled and sliced, divided

2 cups organic apple juice

1 cup spinach

1 teaspoon honey

1 cup ice

1 In a large blender, combine beets, pineapple, 1 kiwi, and apple juice and blend on high until all ingredients are well combined, about 2 minutes.

2 Add spinach and honey and blend on high until all ingredients are well blended, about 1 minute.

3 Add ice gradually while blending on high and blend until smooth.

4 Pour equal amounts of smoothie into each of two serving bowls and garnish each bowl with half the remaining kiwi slices. Serve chilled.

PER SERVING   Calories: 236 | Fat: 0.7 grams | Protein: 2.9 grams | Sodium: 62 milligrams | Fiber: 5.3 grams | Carbohydrates: 58.3 grams | Sugar: 46.7 grams

POWER SOURCES

BEETS: betalain acts as a potent antioxidant to protect cell health against oxidative damage

KIWI: vitamin C supports immune system health

HONEY: antimicrobial compounds combat common germs

SPINACH: fiber supports regular blood sugar levels

☀ POWER BOWL PRIORITIES

Organic foods may cost a little bit more, but when you're trying to achieve optimal health, it's worth it to pay more. Berries, apples, citrus, vegetables, and meats that are nonorganic can be laden with harsh chemicals, pesticides, and additives that can overwhelm the body with toxins that can harm the cells, tissues, organs, and systems' functioning. With organic alternatives, you can keep your body and mind clear of synthetic substances, helping to boost the benefits of every power bowl recipe in this book.

Sweet Potato Quinoa Patties with Creamy Slaw

Prep Time: 15 minutes | **Cook Time:** 10 minutes | **Serves 2**

1 small sweet potato, baked and skin removed, cut into 1" cubes

1 teaspoon salt

1 teaspoon pepper

1 teaspoon garlic powder

¼ teaspoon cayenne

2 tablespoons lime juice

2 tablespoons water

½ cup cooked quinoa

1 tablespoon olive oil

¾ cup nonfat yogurt

2 tablespoons honey

1 tablespoon lemon juice

1 cup peeled and shredded carrots

1 cup shredded cabbage

1. In a blender, combine sweet potato, salt, pepper, garlic powder, cayenne, lime juice, and water. Blend on high until a thick paste develops, about 2 minutes.

2. Move sweet potato mixture to a large bowl and combine with quinoa. Form 4 equally sized patties.

3. Coat a large skillet with olive oil and heat over medium heat. Cook patties for 3–4 minutes on each side until lightly browned. Remove from heat and place patties on paper towels to absorb excess moisture.

4. In a large bowl, combine yogurt, honey, and lemon juice and whisk until thoroughly combined. Add carrots and cabbage and toss to coat.

5. Add equal amounts of slaw to each of two serving bowls and top each with 2 sweet potato patties. Serve warm or chilled.

PER SERVING   Calories: 295 | Fat: 4.5 grams | Protein: 9.7 grams | Sodium: 1319 milligrams | Fiber: 6.2 grams | Carbohydrates: 57.1 grams | Sugar: 31.6 grams

POWER SOURCES

SWEET POTATO: beta carotene acts as an antioxidant for scavenging free radicals from blood

CABBAGE: insoluble fiber cleanses the colon of potentially toxic undigested food particles

YOGURT: calcium and magnesium support the digestive system for improved nutrient absorption

Cucumber-Melon Smoothie with Ginger

Prep Time: 5 minutes | **Cook Time:** N/A | **Serves 2**

- 2 cups cooled green tea
- 1 tablespoon honey
- 1" gingerroot, peeled
- 1 small cucumber, peeled and sliced
- 1 cup cubed cantaloupe
- 1 cup cubed honeydew
- 1 cup spinach
- 2 cups ice
- 2 sprigs fresh mint

1. In a large blender, combine tea, honey, and ginger and blend on high until ginger is emulsified.
2. Add cucumber, melons, and spinach and blend on high until all ingredients are thoroughly combined.
3. Add ice gradually while blending on high and blend until smooth.
4. Pour equal amounts of smoothie into each of two serving bowls. Garnish each bowl with 1 mint leaf. Serve cold.

PER SERVING   Calories: 104 | Fat: 0.2 grams | Protein: 2.1 grams | Sodium: 42 milligrams | Fiber: 2.3 grams | Carbohydrates: 25.7 grams | Sugar: 22.9 grams

POWER SOURCES

CANTALOUPE: lycopene protects brain cells from oxidative damage from free radicals

HONEYDEW MELON: vitamin C protects against free-radical damage

GINGER: anti-inflammatory compounds protect against inflammation

Green Apple–Ginger Smoothie

Prep Time: 5 minutes | **Cook Time:** N/A | **Serves 2**

1 cup spinach

½ cup kale, ribs removed

1 small green apple, peeled and cored

¾" gingerroot, peeled, divided

2 cups unsweetened almond milk

2 cups ice

1 In a blender, combine spinach, kale, green apple, ½" ginger, and almond milk and blend on high until all ingredients are emulsified, about 2–3 minutes.

2 Add ice gradually while blending on high and blend until smooth.

3 Mince remaining ¼" gingerroot.

4 Pour equal amounts of smoothie into each of two serving bowls. Garnish each with half the grated ginger. Serve cold.

PER SERVING   Calories: 76 | Fat: 2.6 grams | Protein: 1.9 grams | Sodium: 173 milligrams | Fiber: 2.5 grams | Carbohydrates: 10.9 grams | Sugar: 7.1 grams

POWER SOURCES

SPINACH: fiber regulates blood sugar spikes that can impede detoxification

KALE: vitamin C ensures healthy immune system functioning

APPLE: quercetin acts as an antioxidant that fights free-radical damage

✳ POWER BOWL PRIORITIES

Whether your goal is to lose weight, have more energy, improve the quality of your sleep, or support your body's systems, metabolism-minded munching can help. By providing your body with unprocessed whole-food power bowls that pack essential vitamins, minerals, and macronutrients into every bite, you can give your metabolic system what it needs to effectively process the foods you eat. Not only does eating power bowls give you the fuel you need to burn fat, produce energy, and sharpen focus, it also improves your body's detoxifying system for a more efficient metabolic processing that continues to improve over time.

Waldorf Chicken Salad Lettuce Cups

Prep Time: 10 minutes | **Cook Time:** N/A | **Serves 2**

1 (4-ounce) grilled chicken breast

3 stalks celery, chopped

1 small cucumber, peeled and chopped

½ cup halved seedless green grapes

½ cup halved seedless red grapes

1½ cups nonfat yogurt

6 large leaves Bibb lettuce

½ cup raw oats

½ cup crushed walnuts

1 tablespoon honey

1. In a large bowl, shred chicken and add celery, cucumber, and grapes. Toss to combine.
2. Add yogurt and toss to coat thoroughly.
3. Place 3 lettuce leaves in each of two serving bowls and fill with equal amounts of chicken salad mixture.
4. In a small bowl, combine oats, walnuts, and honey and stir to combine thoroughly.
5. Sprinkle each lettuce cup with half the oat mixture. Serve chilled.

PER SERVING   Calories: 538 | Fat: 20.6 grams | Protein: 31.8 grams | Sodium: 195 milligrams | Fiber: 6.7 grams | Carbohydrates: 58.5 grams | Sugar: 37.6 grams

POWER SOURCES

CHICKEN: vitamin B$_{12}$ promotes healthy red blood cell production

GRAPES: resveratrol acts as an antioxidant to scavenge free radicals from blood

WALNUTS: vitamin E acts as an antioxidant to detox the body of potential cancer-causing agents

Minty Mango-Grape Cream Smoothie

Prep Time: 5 minutes | **Cook Time:** N/A | **Serves 2**

1 cup seedless purple grapes

1 cup peeled and cubed mango

1 tablespoon fresh mint leaves plus 4 mint leaves, divided

1 cup cooled white tea

1 cup nonfat yogurt

2 cups ice

POWER SOURCES

MANGO: vitamin C supports healthy immune system functioning

YOGURT: probiotics support immunity by promoting gut health

WHITE TEA: natural phytochemicals promote lipolysis for fat metabolism and detoxification

1. In a large blender, combine grapes, mango, 1 tablespoon mint leaves, and white tea and blend on high until all ingredients are emulsified, about 1–2 minutes.

2. Add yogurt and blend on high until all ingredients are well blended, about 1–2 minutes.

3. Add ice gradually while blending on high and blend until smooth.

4. Pour equal amounts of smoothie into each of two serving bowls and garnish each bowl with 2 fresh mint leaves. Serve cold.

PER SERVING   Calories: 171 | Fat: 0.5 grams | Protein: 8.3 grams | Sodium: 99 milligrams | Fiber: 2.1 grams | Carbohydrates: 35.9 grams | Sugar: 32.4 grams

Salmon with Asparagus and Almonds over Brown Rice

Prep Time: 15 minutes | **Cook Time:** 15 minutes | **Serves 2**

2 tablespoons olive oil, divided

½ pound asparagus spears, ends trimmed

2 (6-ounce) salmon fillets

4 lemon slices

2 tablespoons crushed tarragon

2 tablespoons lemon juice

1 cup cooked brown rice

¼ cup slivered almonds

POWER SOURCES

SALMON: omega-3s support blood health by reducing triglycerides

ASPARAGUS: glutathione acts as a potent antioxidant to prevent free-radical damage in cells

LEMON: vitamin C supports cell, tissue, and organ health throughout detoxification

BROWN RICE: fiber promotes stable blood sugar levels and liver functioning

1 Preheat oven to 400°F.

2 Drizzle ½ tablespoon olive oil into each of two 12" × 12" foil packages. In each pouch, place half the asparagus and top with 1 salmon fillet. Cover each salmon fillet with 2 lemon slices and 1 tablespoon tarragon; drizzle ½ tablespoon olive oil over top of each fillet. Pour 1 tablespoon lemon juice into each pouch. Close pouches by bringing opposite right and left ends together and opposite top and bottom ends to enclose and contain heat.

3 Bake salmon in pouches for 15 minutes or until flaky and cooked through. Remove from heat.

4 Place ½ cup rice in each of two serving bowls and top each with the contents of a pouch. Drizzle juices from pouches over top of each bowl. Garnish each bowl with ⅛ cup slivered almonds. Serve hot or cold.

PER SERVING   Calories: 531 | Fat: 22.5 grams | Protein: 43.6 grams | Sodium: 132 milligrams | Fiber: 6.2 grams | Carbohydrates: 33.7 grams | Sugar: 3.1 grams

Peach-Cherry-Tofu Chutney with Creamy Quinoa

Prep Time: 15 minutes | **Cook Time:** 25 minutes | **Serves 2**

2 small peaches, pitted and sliced

½ pound pitted cherries

½ cup water

2 tablespoons olive oil

8 ounces extra-firm tofu, cut into ¼" cubes

1 teaspoon salt

1 teaspoon pepper

1 cup cooked quinoa

1 cup nonfat Greek yogurt

POWER SOURCES

PEACH: vitamin A acts as an antioxidant to promote healthy cellular functioning

CHERRIES: anthocyanins act to scavenge free radicals from the blood

TOFU: vegetable-based protein promotes easy digestion

1 In a large saucepan over medium heat, combine peaches, cherries, and water. Simmer for 5 minutes or until peaches are fork-tender; mash cherries and peaches. Bring mixture to a boil and reduce to a simmer until a somewhat thick sauce is produced, about 5–7 minutes. Remove from heat.

2 Coat a large skillet with olive oil and heat over medium heat. Then sprinkle tofu with salt and pepper and sauté for 5–7 minutes or until golden brown. Add mashed peaches and cherries and quinoa and sauté for 2–3 minutes or until heated through.

3 In a large bowl, combine the quinoa mixture and yogurt and stir until thoroughly combined.

4 Pour equal amounts of quinoa mixture into each of two serving bowls. Spoon half the chutney over top of each bowl. Serve warm or chilled.

PER SERVING   Calories: 389 | Fat: 12.6 grams | Protein: 19.2 grams | Sodium: 1219 milligrams | Fiber: 6.8 grams | Carbohydrates: 52.7 grams | Sugar: 28.1 grams

Rice Noodles with Peaches and Berries

Prep Time: 10 minutes | **Cook Time:** 15 minutes | **Serves 2**

4 cups water

8 ounces uncooked rice noodles

2 small peaches, pitted and sliced

½ cup blueberries

½ cup raspberries

2 tablespoons lemon juice

1 cup nonfat Greek yogurt

2 tablespoons honey

POWER SOURCES

PEACH: vitamin A provides powerful antioxidant protection

BLUEBERRIES: anthocyanins prevent cellular degradation resulting from oxidative stress

HONEY: natural antioxidants support cell health while removing free radicals from blood and tissue

1   In a large saucepot, bring 4 cups water to a boil over high heat. Stir in rice noodles and cook until al dente, about 3–5 minutes. Remove from heat, drain, and place in a large bowl to cool.

2   In the same pot, combine peaches, blueberries, raspberries, and lemon juice. Heat over medium heat and bring to a simmer. Cook until fruits are fork-tender, about 8–10 minutes. Remove from heat.

3   Add yogurt and honey to the bowl of rice noodles and stir to coat completely.

4   Pour equal amounts of rice noodles into each of two serving bowls and top each with equal amounts of peach and berry mixture. Serve hot or cold.

PER SERVING   Calories: 619 | Fat: 0.9 grams | Protein: 19.9 grams | Sodium: 253 milligrams | Fiber: 6.2 grams | Carbohydrates: 131.8 grams | Sugar: 35.2 grams

Spicy Cilantro-Citrus Salmon with Rice

Prep Time: 10 minutes | **Cook Time:** 15 minutes | **Serves 2**

2 tablespoons olive oil, divided

2 (6-ounce) salmon fillets

1 teaspoon salt

1 teaspoon pepper

¼ cup chopped fresh cilantro

1 cup chopped spinach

1 small grapefruit, seeded, peeled, and sliced

¼ teaspoon cayenne

1 cup prepared brown rice

1 Preheat oven to 400°F and grease two 12" × 12" aluminum foil pieces with 1 tablespoon olive oil.

2 Lay 1 salmon fillet on each piece of prepared foil and sprinkle each fillet with ½ teaspoon salt and ½ teaspoon pepper. Top each packet with ⅛ cup cilantro, ½ cup spinach, and half the grapefruit sections. Sprinkle each pouch with ⅛ teaspoon cayenne. Bake for 15 minutes or until salmon is cooked through and flaky. Remove from heat.

3 Place ½ cup brown rice in each of two serving bowls and top each with the salmon contents of each aluminum pouch, drizzling with juices remaining. Serve hot or chilled.

PER SERVING   Calories: 452 | Fat: 15.8 grams | Protein: 38.4 grams | Sodium: 1302 milligrams | Fiber: 3.6 grams | Carbohydrates: 32.5 grams | Sugar: 7.1 grams

POWER SOURCES

CILANTRO: manganese is part of many enzymes aiding in metabolism, which helps rid the body of toxins produced during those reactions

SALMON: omega-3s promote brain functions related to energy and hormones

BROWN RICE: insoluble fiber promotes sustained energy throughout detox

CHAPTER 6
Bowls for Better Immunity

By helping to prevent the onset of illness and disease while making sure your body functions at an optimal level, the immune system is responsible for both your level of health and your quality (and duration!) of life. And a diet full of the power bowl recipes in this chapter directly affects your immune system by giving you essential vitamins, minerals, and phytonutrients that can help your body not only function but thrive!

These immunity-boosting power bowls are full of hardworking, nutrient-dense foods like citrus fruits, sweet potatoes, and peppers and calcium-rich additions that pack each and every bowl with rich flavors and the immense nutrition that comes from eating a rainbow of fruits and veggies. These vegetables and fruits add a wide variety of essential vitamins, minerals, and protective antioxidants to every dish, which will support your immune system functioning while also safeguarding your cells against free radicals and oxidative damage. With whole grains providing the body and brain with clean carbohydrates and proteins that support your immune system, these power bowls naturally pack every last bite with delicious nutrition that improves overall health and maximizes immune system protection.

Spicy Pineapple Skillet

Prep Time: 5 minutes | **Cook Time:** 10 minutes | **Serves 2**

1 tablespoon olive oil

8 ounces extra-firm tofu, sliced into ¼" pieces

¼ teaspoon cayenne

½ cup pomegranate jewels

1 cup chopped pineapple

1 tablespoon lemon juice

4 cups arugula

1. Coat a large skillet with olive oil and heat over medium heat. Add tofu slices and cook 3–5 minutes or until golden. Then flip the tofu and sprinkle with cayenne.

2. Add pomegranate jewels, pineapple, and lemon juice. Cook 3 minutes, then remove from heat.

3. Place 2 cups arugula in each of two serving bowls and layer equal portions of tofu, pineapple, and pomegranate over top. Serve hot.

PER SERVING   Calories: 236 | Fat: 11.4 grams | Protein: 13.5 grams | Sodium: 21 milligrams | Fiber: 4.1 grams | Carbohydrates: 23.3 grams | Sugar: 15.7 grams

POWER SOURCES

CAYENNE: capsaicin acts as a powerful antioxidant for maximized immune system functioning

POMEGRANATE: vitamin K acts to promote tissue and organ health with antioxidant protection

ARUGULA: potassium promotes circulatory-system health

Peach-Berry Crumble

Prep Time: 5 minutes | **Cook Time:** 10 minutes | **Serves 2**

2 cups dry rolled oats

1 cup blueberries

1 cup raspberries

2 tablespoons coconut oil

1 tablespoon honey

1 cup nonfat vanilla yogurt

2 small peaches, pitted and sliced

1 Preheat oven to 400°F.

2 In a large bowl, toss oats, berries, oil, and honey until evenly coated.

3 Place oat mixture on a baking sheet and bake for 5 minutes.

4 Turn oats and berries and cook for 5 minutes or until oats are crisp.

5 Remove from oven, add to a large bowl, and toss thoroughly.

6 Pour equal amounts of oat-berry mixture into each of two serving bowls and top each with ½ cup yogurt and half the peach slices. Serve hot or cold.

PER SERVING   Calories: 615 | Fat: 17.9 grams | Protein: 17.3 grams | Sodium: 72 milligrams | Fiber: 15.4 grams | Carbohydrates: 99.2 grams | Sugar: 36.1 grams

POWER SOURCES

PEACH: vitamin A acts as a potent antioxidant that protects your cells from free-radical damage

BLUEBERRIES: manganese supports neuromuscular health and prevents bone loss

RASPBERRIES: vitamin C prevents and reverses cell degradation from harmful oxidative processes

HONEY: antimicrobial and antifungal compounds provide protection for the immune system

Lemon Chicken with Figs and Greens

Prep Time: 10 minutes | **Cook Time:** 20 minutes | **Serves 2**

- 1 tablespoon olive oil
- 2 (4-ounce) chicken breasts, halved lengthwise
- 3 medium figs, pitted and sliced
- 2 tablespoons lemon juice
- 2 cups kale, ribs removed
- 2 cups spinach
- 2 tablespoons chopped rosemary
- 2 cups cooked brown rice
- 2 tablespoons reduced-fat feta cheese

1. Coat a large skillet with olive oil and heat over medium heat.
2. Add chicken breasts and cook for 7–9 minutes or until golden brown.
3. Flip chicken breasts and add figs, lemon juice, and kale to skillet. Cook for 7 minutes or until kale is cooked through and chicken juices run clear. Remove from heat and stir in spinach and rosemary until spinach is wilted and rosemary is evenly distributed throughout, about 1 minute.
4. Place 1 cup brown rice in each of two serving bowls and layer each with equal amounts of chicken mixture. Sprinkle 1 tablespoon feta over top of each bowl. Serve hot.

PER SERVING Calories: 480 | Fat: 9.7 grams | Protein: 32.7 grams | Sodium: 138 milligrams | Fiber: 8.4 grams | Carbohydrates: 66.1 grams | Sugar: 13.1 grams

POWER SOURCES

LEMON: vitamin C strengthens and supports the functioning of the immune system

ROSEMARY: carnosic acid provides antioxidant protection to the blood and tissues

SPINACH: iron promotes blood health by supporting red blood cell production and repair

✳ POWER BOWL PRIORITIES

While most combinations of fruits require little sweetening—if any at all—you may be surprised by how much more flavorful those fruity combinations can be when you add a little lemon or lime. The citric acid and strong acidity of these two fruits brighten and heighten flavors for even greater sweetness. With the additional polyphenols that act as potent antioxidants for improved health and immunity, these sensational fruits do double duty for flavor and health.

Oriental Chicken Salad with Mandarin Dressing

Prep Time: 10 minutes | **Cook Time:** N/A | **Serves 2**

2 (4-ounce) grilled chicken breasts

4 mandarin oranges, seeded, peeled, and segmented

¼ cup sesame seeds

½ cup cranberries

2 tablespoons sesame oil

2 tablespoons rice wine vinegar

4 cups chopped spinach

1 cup cooked quinoa

1 Tear chicken into bite-sized pieces and place in a large bowl. Add oranges, sesame seeds, cranberries, sesame oil, and vinegar. Toss to combine.

2 Place 2 cups spinach in each of two serving bowls and top each with ½ cup quinoa. Spoon equal amounts of chicken and fruit mixture over each. Serve chilled.

PER SERVING   Calories: 613 | Fat: 27.0 grams | Protein: 44.9 grams | Sodium: 117 milligrams | Fiber: 9.9 grams | Carbohydrates: 49.6 grams | Sugar: 18.3 grams

POWER SOURCES

MANDARIN ORANGE: vitamin C assists in immune system functioning and protects cell health

CHICKEN: when consumed with a carbohydrate, lean protein helps stabilize blood sugar and prevent insulin spikes

SESAME SEEDS: zinc provides optimal immune system functioning

Spiced Salsa Sweet Potatoes

Prep Time: 10 minutes | **Cook Time:** 30 minutes | **Serves 2**

2 large sweet potatoes

2 large tomatoes, chopped

1 small Vidalia onion, peeled and chopped

2 garlic cloves, minced

¼ cup chopped fresh cilantro

½ (8-ounce) can black beans, rinsed and drained

1 small jalapeño, seeded and minced

1 teaspoon salt

1 Preheat oven to 400°F and bake sweet potatoes until fork-tender, about 30 minutes.

2 In a small bowl, combine tomatoes, onion, garlic, cilantro, black beans, jalapeño, and salt and stir to combine thoroughly.

3 Place 1 sweet potato into each of two serving bowls and slice lengthwise to open skin.

4 Top each with equal amounts of salsa. Serve hot or chilled.

PER SERVING   Calories: 212 | Fat: 0.3 grams | Protein: 7.8 grams | Sodium: 1300 milligrams | Fiber: 10.2 grams | Carbohydrates: 46.9 grams | Sugar: 17.6 grams

POWER SOURCES

ONION: chromium aids in glucose regulation

CILANTRO: manganese's antioxidant properties support healthy cell functioning and promotes immunity

SWEET POTATO: B vitamins and vitamin C combine to promote immune system and cardiac functions

Dandelion-Pesto Chicken with Tomatoes and Arugula

Prep Time: 10 minutes | **Cook Time:** 20 minutes | **Serves 2**

1 cup chopped dandelion greens

2 garlic cloves

¼ cup shredded Parmesan cheese

1 teaspoon salt

1 teaspoon pepper

¼ cup plus 1 tablespoon olive oil, divided

2 (4-ounce) chicken breasts

2 cups cherry tomatoes

2 cups cooked quinoa

2 cups chopped arugula

2 tablespoons balsamic vinegar

1   Preheat oven to 375°F.

2   In a blender, combine dandelion greens, garlic, Parmesan, salt, pepper, and ¼ cup oil and blend on high until all ingredients are emulsified and well blended, about 1–2 minutes.

3   Place chicken breasts in a 13" × 9" pan. Dress breasts with dandelion pesto and surround chicken with cherry tomatoes. Bake for 20 minutes or until chicken is cooked through and juices run clear. Remove from heat.

4   In a large bowl, toss together quinoa, arugula, remaining 1 tablespoon olive oil, and vinegar until well combined and thoroughly coated.

5   Layer equal amounts of quinoa mixture into each of two serving bowls and top each with 1 chicken breast and half the tomatoes. Serve hot.

POWER SOURCES

OLIVE OIL: monounsaturated fats promote healthy metabolic functioning

GARLIC: allicin acts as an antimicrobial that protects the body from germs and illness

TOMATO: vitamin A helps support the normal function of immune-related cells

PER SERVING   Calories: 745 | Fat: 40.8 grams | Protein: 39.0 grams | Sodium: 1381 milligrams | Fiber: 8.6 grams | Carbohydrates: 53.3 grams | Sugar: 8.6 grams

Tropical-Fruit Compote Tofu Salad

Prep Time: 10 minutes | **Cook Time:** 15 minutes | **Serves 2**

- 3 tablespoons coconut oil, divided
- 8 ounces extra-firm tofu, sliced thin
- 4 cups spinach
- 2 cups cooked bulgur
- 1 cup chopped pineapple
- 1 small pink grapefruit, seeded, peeled, and sliced
- 1 small orange, seeded, peeled, and sliced
- 1 teaspoon salt
- 1 teaspoon pepper

1 Coat a large skillet with 2 tablespoons coconut oil and heat over medium heat. Add tofu and cook for 4–7 minutes on each side or until golden brown. Remove from heat.

2 In a large bowl, combine tofu and spinach and toss to combine.

3 Place 1 cup bulgur in each of two serving bowls and top each with equal amounts of the spinach and tofu mixture. Spoon equal amounts of pineapple, grapefruit, and orange into each bowl. Drizzle each bowl with ½ tablespoon coconut oil and season each bowl with ½ teaspoon salt and ½ teaspoon pepper. Serve warm.

PER SERVING   Calories: 541 | Fat: 21.2 grams | Protein: 21.1 grams | Sodium: 1228 milligrams | Fiber: 15.1 grams | Carbohydrates: 74.8 grams | Sugar: 30.4 grams

POWER SOURCES

PINEAPPLE: vitamin C acts as an antioxidant to support immune system functioning

GRAPEFRUIT: lycopene protects heart health

SPINACH: iron supports blood health and promotes cardiovascular functioning

Ginger-Infused Green Tea Ice Cream

Prep Time: 2 hours | **Cook Time:** N/A | **Serves 2**

2 cups cooled green tea

1" gingerroot, peeled

2 tablespoons aloe vera juice

1 tablespoon apple cider vinegar

2 tablespoons honey

2 cups nonfat yogurt

1 cup ice

2 sprigs fresh mint

1 In a blender, combine green tea and ginger and blend on high until ginger is emulsified, about 1 minute.

2 Add aloe vera, apple cider vinegar, honey, and yogurt and blend on high until thoroughly combined. Add ice while blending on high and blend until thick and smooth, about 1–2 minutes.

3 Pour half of blender into each of two serving bowls and freeze for 2 hours or until solidified and creamy. Garnish each bowl with 1 sprig of mint. Serve cold.

PER SERVING Calories: 214 | Fat: 0.4 grams | Protein: 14.2 grams | Sodium: 190 milligrams | Fiber: 0.1 grams | Carbohydrates: 39.0 grams | Sugar: 37.7 grams

POWER SOURCES

GINGER: gingerol is thought to act as a potent anti-inflammatory agent

GREEN TEA: natural antioxidants protect against cell damage and DNA damage

APPLE CIDER VINEGAR: antimicrobial and antiviral enzymes protect against illness

Mediterranean Veggie Burgers with Cucumber-Dill Cream

Prep Time: 10 minutes | **Cook Time:** 15 minutes | **Serves 2**

1 (8-ounce) can garbanzo beans, rinsed and drained

½ cup olives, pitted

1 small red bell pepper, ribs removed, seeded, and sliced

1 cup spinach

¼ cup olive oil

2 cloves garlic

1 cup cooked barley

2 tablespoons olive oil

1 small cucumber, peeled and chopped

1 cup Greek yogurt

¼ cup chopped fresh dill

1 teaspoon garlic powder

1 teaspoon salt

1 In a food processor, combine beans, olives, red pepper, spinach, olive oil, and garlic and blend on high until all ingredients are emulsified and a paste develops, about 2–3 minutes.

2 In a large bowl, toss bean mixture with barley until well combined and form 4 patties.

3 Coat a large skillet with olive oil and heat over medium heat. Add patties and cook for 5–7 minutes on each side or until crispy. Remove from heat.

4 In a food processor, combine cucumber, yogurt, dill, garlic powder, and salt and blend to combine thoroughly, about 1–2 minutes.

5 Place 2 patties in each of two serving bowls and top each with equal amounts of cucumber cream.

PER SERVING Calories: 814 | Fat: 49.2 grams | Protein: 25.0 grams | Sodium: 1737 milligrams | Fiber: 16.4 grams | Carbohydrates: 71.0 grams | Sugar: 12.1 grams

POWER SOURCES

CUCUMBER: manganese prevents inflammation and supports heart health

GARBANZO BEANS: fiber and protein promote healthy digestive processes for improved nutrient absorption and immune system defense

BELL PEPPER: vitamin A acts as a potent antioxidant fighting free-radical damage

Spiced Cherry Cream Smoothie Bowl

Prep Time: 5 minutes | **Cook Time:** N/A | **Serves 2**

2 cups pitted cherries plus 4 whole cherries, divided

½" gingerroot, peeled

1 cup low-fat canned coconut milk

2 cups nonfat yogurt

2 tablespoons honey

1 teaspoon cinnamon

1 teaspoon cardamom

1 cup ice

2 tablespoons flaxseed

1 In a large blender, combine pitted cherries, ginger, and coconut milk and blend on high until ingredients are emulsified and well blended.

2 Add yogurt, honey, cinnamon, and cardamom and blend on high until thoroughly combined. Add ice gradually while blending on high and blend until smooth.

3 Pour equal amounts of smoothie into each of two serving bowls. Garnish each bowl with 2 whole cherries and 1 tablespoon flaxseed. Serve cold.

PER SERVING   Calories: 468 | Fat: 13.8 grams | Protein: 18.0 grams | Sodium: 218 milligrams | Fiber: 7.3 grams | Carbohydrates: 69.5 grams | Sugar: 59.5 grams

POWER SOURCES

CHERRIES: flavonoids combat free-radical damage and cleanse blood of impurities

CINNAMON: antimicrobial agents help to boost immunity by protecting against illness

YOGURT: probiotics promote gut health and growth of healthy bacteria

Sweet Salmon Salad

Prep Time: 10 minutes | **Cook Time:** 15 minutes | **Serves 2**

2 (6-ounce) salmon fillets

2 tablespoons honey

1 teaspoon salt

1 cup chopped kale

1 cup chopped purple cabbage

2 cups spinach

4 tablespoons olive oil

2 tablespoons balsamic vinegar

1 Preheat oven to 400°F. Layer salmon fillets in a baking dish, drizzle with honey, and season with salt. Bake for 15 minutes or until cooked through. Remove from heat.

2 In a large bowl, combine kale, cabbage, spinach, olive oil, and vinegar. Toss to coat.

3 Layer equal amounts of salad in each of two serving bowls and top each with 1 cooked salmon fillet. Serve hot or chilled.

PER SERVING   Calories: 523 | Fat: 28.1 grams | Protein: 36.8 grams | Sodium: 1328 milligrams | Fiber: 2.1 grams | Carbohydrates: 24.1 grams | Sugar: 21.1 grams

POWER SOURCES

SALMON: omega-3s provide antioxidant protection for cells and blood

HONEY: antifungal properties promote immunity against internal and external fungal effects

OLIVE OIL: healthy fats support brain functioning and promote healthy weight maintenance for improved overall health

☀ POWER BOWL PRIORITIES

Cabbage of all colors contains a unique phytochemical that has been shown to have remarkable results in cancer prevention. With sinigrin, a glucosinolate that can be converted to allyl isothiocyanate (AITC), cabbage provides the body with useful compounds that combat cancerous cellular changes in the bladder, colon, and prostate. A healthy and delicious addition to slaws, smoothies, and any other type of power bowl, cabbage is a great way to be cancer-free naturally!

CHAPTER 7
Bowls for Brain Health

Whether you're hoping to improve mental functions like cognitive processes and memory, or hoping to prevent serious illness and disease such as dementia and Alzheimer's, eating for better brain health is essential. The nutritious foods that are contained in each and every one of the power bowl recipes in this chapter make eating for better brain health a simply delicious task. Here, brain food gets dressed up in smoothies, salads, and entrées that combine omega-rich foods like salmon and flaxseed with whole grains, vegetables, fruits, and delicious additions that all work together to support and promote healthy brain functioning. And with essential nutrients like iron, potassium, and magnesium; B vitamins; and antioxidants; the body and brain are able to work as designed.

With delicious meal and snack options that make breakfast, lunch, or dinner the perfect time to boost brain health, power bowls provide outstanding nutrition with a delicious delivery. Brain food never tasted so good!

Grilled Chicken with Peach Couscous Salad and Cranberries

Prep Time: 10 minutes | **Cook Time:** 15 minutes | **Serves 2**

1 (4-ounce) chicken breast, halved lengthwise

1 teaspoon salt

4 cups chopped spinach

1 cup chopped arugula

2 cups cooked couscous

1 cup dried cranberries

2 small peaches, pitted and sliced

1 tablespoon olive oil

1 tablespoon red wine vinegar

1 Set a grill to medium-high heat and place chicken breast halves on grill surface. Season with salt and cook for 5–7 minutes on each side until cooked through and juices run clear. Remove from heat and cut into strips.

2 In a large bowl, combine spinach, arugula, couscous, and cranberries and toss to thoroughly combine.

3 Add half the salad and half the chicken breast strips to each of two serving bowls. Top each bowl with slices of 1 peach. Drizzle each bowl with ½ tablespoon oil and ½ tablespoon vinegar. Serve warm.

PER SERVING   Calories: 536 | Fat: 8.4 grams | Protein: 21.0 grams | Sodium: 1221 milligrams | Fiber: 8.6 grams | Carbohydrates: 98.2 grams | Sugar: 48.2 grams

POWER SOURCES

CHICKEN: B_{12} promotes mood-related hormone production in the brain

PEACH: beta carotene acts as a potent antioxidant for brain cell health protection against degenerative disease

SPINACH: iron improves the ability of oxygen to bind to red blood cells for transport throughout the body

Superfood Chili

Prep Time: 10 minutes | **Cook Time:** 25 minutes | **Serves 4**

2 tablespoons olive oil

8 ounces extra-firm tofu, crumbled

1 small yellow onion, peeled and chopped

1 cup canned, rinsed, and drained black beans

1 cup canned, rinsed, and drained garbanzo beans

1 cup canned, rinsed, and drained kidney beans

2 small tomatoes, chopped

2 garlic cloves, minced

2 teaspoons salt

1/4 teaspoon cayenne

2 cups cooked quinoa

1/2 cup Greek yogurt

1/2 cup shredded Cheddar cheese

1 Drizzle olive oil into a large pot and heat over medium heat. Add tofu crumbles and onions. Cook until tofu is golden brown and onions are opaque, 7–9 minutes.

2 Add all beans, tomatoes, and garlic; season with salt and cayenne and stir to combine thoroughly. Cook for 10 minutes.

3 Add quinoa and mix until well combined. Heat through for 5 minutes.

4 Pour equal amounts of chili into each of two serving bowls. Top each bowl with 1/4 cup Greek yogurt and 1/4 cup shredded Cheddar. Serve hot.

PER SERVING   Calories: 478 | Fat: 17.9 grams | Protein: 26.5 grams | Sodium: 1518 milligrams | Fiber: 13.4 grams | Carbohydrates: 52.4 grams | Sugar: 6.7 grams

POWER SOURCES

BLACK BEANS: fiber promotes healthy blood sugar levels for optimal cognitive functioning

GARBANZO BEANS: protein supports enzymatic activities within the central nervous system

TOMATO: lycopene safeguards cells against degenerative disease

TOFU: soy protein provides phytonutrients that support the repair process of cells

Lox Salad with Berries

Prep Time: 5 minutes | **Cook Time:** N/A | **Serves 2**

4 cups spinach

2 tablespoons ground flaxseed

2 tablespoons olive oil

2 tablespoons balsamic vinegar

1 cup blueberries

1 cup raspberries

1 cup sliced strawberries, tops removed

8 ounces thinly sliced lox

1 In a large bowl, combine spinach, flaxseed, olive oil, and balsamic vinegar. Toss to coat.

2 Add berries and toss to combine.

3 Pour equal amounts of the dressed salad into each of two serving bowls and top each with 4 ounces sliced lox. Serve cold.

PER SERVING   Calories: 401 | Fat: 19.5 grams | Protein: 25.6 grams | Sodium: 2321 milligrams | Fiber: 10.7 grams | Carbohydrates: 31.4 grams | Sugar: 16.9 grams

POWER SOURCES

LOX: omega-3s promote brain health

SPINACH: vitamin K helps with blood clotting

STRAWBERRIES: anthocyanins promote health of organs and cells

Ginger-Salmon with Wild Rice and Vegetables

Prep Time: 5 minutes | **Cook Time:** 25 minutes | **Serves 2**

1 tablespoon olive oil

2 (6-ounce) salmon fillets

1" gingerroot, peeled and grated

1 tablespoon lemon juice

1 tablespoon honey

1 large zucchini, sliced

1 small Vidalia onion, peeled and sliced

½ cup halved cherry tomatoes

1 teaspoon salt

2 cups cooked wild rice

1 Preheat oven to 400°F and grease a 13" × 9" baking pan with olive oil. Add salmon fillets and ginger and drizzle with lemon juice and honey. Surround salmon fillets with zucchini, onion, and tomatoes and season entire pan with salt.

2 Bake for 25 minutes or until salmon is cooked through and flaky.

3 Place 1 cup wild rice in each of two serving bowls. Top each bowl with 1 salmon fillet and half the vegetables. Serve hot or cold.

PER SERVING   Calories: 520 | Fat: 12.5 grams | Protein: 44.1 grams | Sodium: 1309 milligrams | Fiber: 5.6 grams | Carbohydrates: 53.6 grams | Sugar: 16.3 grams

POWER SOURCES

SALMON: omega-3s support nerve cell sheath composition for improved communication in the brain

WILD RICE: fiber promotes low cholesterol levels in the blood

ZUCCHINI: provides essential B vitamins for optimal hormone production and balance

TOMATO: potassium supports healthy nerve function

Jalapeño-Apricot Tofu with Peppers and Noodles

Prep Time: 10 minutes | **Cook Time:** 15 minutes | **Serves 2**

1 tablespoon olive oil

8 ounces extra-firm tofu, sliced into ¼"-thick fillets

½ small red bell pepper, seeded and cut into strips

½ small green bell pepper, seeded and cut into strips

1 small jalapeño, seeded and chopped

1 teaspoon salt

1 teaspoon garlic powder

8 ounces cooked rice noodles

4 dried apricots, chopped

1 Coat a large skillet with olive oil and heat over medium-high heat. Add tofu and cook for 3–5 minutes on each side or until golden brown. Remove tofu from pan and set aside.

2 Add peppers and jalapeño to skillet and cook for 5 minutes or until slightly softened; return tofu to skillet and season with salt and garlic powder. Remove from heat.

3 Place even amounts of noodles in each of two serving bowls and top each with half the tofu, half the peppers, and half the apricots. Serve warm.

PER SERVING   Calories: 308 | Fat: 11.2 grams | Protein: 14.2 grams | Sodium: 1194 milligrams | Fiber: 3.2 grams | Carbohydrates: 39.3 grams | Sugar: 7.9 grams

POWER SOURCES

APRICOT: beta carotene provides antioxidant protection against cancerous changes in cells

BELL PEPPER: vitamin C promotes eye health

OLIVE OIL: monounsaturated fats help protect against cognitive decline when replacing saturated fats in the diet

TOFU: proteins contribute to the proper metabolism of energy for cells

Coconut-Crusted Mahi-Mahi with Edamame Salad

Prep Time: 10 minutes | **Cook Time:** 15 minutes | **Serves 2**

2 tablespoons olive oil

½ cup unsweetened coconut flakes

2 (6-ounce) mahi-mahi fillets

½ cup grapefruit juice

2 cups chopped kale

2 tablespoons lemon juice

1 cup water

2 cups cooked wild rice

1 cup shelled and cooked edamame

1 teaspoon salt

1 teaspoon pepper

1 Coat a large skillet with olive oil and heat over medium heat. Add coconut flakes to a small bowl, dredge fish to coat completely, and add to pan. Add grapefruit juice; cook 5 minutes on each side or until coconut is golden brown and fish is cooked through.

2 Add kale, lemon juice, and water to skillet and steam until kale is wilted, about 5 minutes. Remove from heat.

3 In a large bowl, toss rice and edamame until thoroughly combined.

4 Layer equal amounts of the rice-edamame mixture in each of two serving bowls and top each with half the kale and 1 mahi-mahi fillet; season each bowl with ½ teaspoon salt and ½ teaspoon pepper. Serve hot.

PER SERVING   Calories: 615 | Fat: 23.4 grams | Protein: 46.8 grams | Sodium: 1324 milligrams | Fiber: 10.3 grams | Carbohydrates: 54.8 grams | Sugar: 10.2 grams

POWER SOURCES

COCONUT: phytochemicals provide antiaging benefits

MAHI-MAHI: protein supports red blood cell production for essential oxygen transport to the brain

EDAMAME: vitamin K supports calcium retainment in bones

KALE: vitamin C combats free-radical damage to cells

Sweet Salmon with Garlic Zucchini Noodles

Prep Time: 10 minutes | **Cook Time:** 20 minutes | **Serves 2**

1 large zucchini

2 tablespoons olive oil, divided

1 garlic clove, minced

¼ cup chopped fresh cilantro

1 teaspoon salt

2 (6-ounce) salmon fillets

¼ cup chopped pineapple

POWER SOURCES

GARLIC: allicin combats bacteria and viruses that can impact brain functioning

SALMON: provides DHA (docosahexaenoic acid, an omega-3 fatty acid) for improved memory and cognition

ZUCCHINI: potassium helps regulate blood pressure

CILANTRO: vitamin A works as an antioxidant to help support a healthy immune system

1 Use a spiralizer to create thin zucchini noodles (size of preference). In a large bowl, toss zucchini noodles with 1 tablespoon olive oil, garlic, and cilantro and season with salt. Set aside.

2 Preheat oven to 375°F and grease a 13" × 9" glass dish with remaining 1 tablespoon oil. Set salmon fillets in dish and cover with pineapple chunks. Bake for 15–20 minutes or until fillets are fully cooked and flaky. Remove from heat.

3 Serve equal amounts of zucchini noodles into each of two serving bowls and top each bowl with 1 salmon fillet and ⅛ cup pineapple.

PER SERVING   Calories: 328 | Fat: 13.5 grams | Protein: 37.0 grams | Sodium: 1302 milligrams | Fiber: 1.9 grams | Carbohydrates: 8.1 grams | Sugar: 5.9 grams

Mixed Greens with Quinoa, Eggs, and Peppers

Prep Time: 10 minutes | **Cook Time:** N/A | **Serves 2**

1 cup cooked quinoa

½ small orange bell pepper, seeded and chopped

½ small red onion, peeled and minced

2 tablespoons olive oil

1 tablespoon balsamic vinegar

4 cups mixed greens

2 large hard-boiled eggs, peeled and halved

1 In a large bowl, combine quinoa, peppers, onions, oil and vinegar. Toss to thoroughly combine and evenly coat.

2 Place 2 cups greens in each of two serving bowls and top each with half the quinoa mixture and 2 hard-boiled egg halves. Serve chilled.

PER SERVING   Calories: 326 | Fat: 17.6 grams | Protein: 12.3 grams | Sodium: 136 milligrams | Fiber: 4.6 grams | Carbohydrates: 31.0 grams | Sugar: 3.2 grams

POWER SOURCES

EGG: choline supports healthy brain functions like cognition and memory maintenance

BELL PEPPER: vitamin A fights free radical damage in cells

QUINOA: amino acids promote hormone levels that improve sleep patterns for better brain functioning

Green Tropical Smoothie with Banana and Berries

Prep Time: 5 minutes | **Cook Time:** N/A | **Serves 2**

1 cup chopped pineapple

½ cup spinach

2½ cups Coconutmilk (I prefer Silk brand)

1¼ cups blueberries, divided

1 medium banana, peeled and chopped

3 tablespoons ground flaxseed, divided

1 cup ice

1 In a large blender, combine pineapple, spinach, and Coconutmilk and blend on high until pineapple and spinach are emulsified, about 3 minutes.

2 Add 1 cup blueberries and banana and blend on high until thoroughly combined.

3 Add 2 tablespoons flaxseed and blend until well incorporated.

4 Add ice gradually while blending on high and blend until smooth. Pour equal amounts of smoothie into each of two serving bowls. Sprinkle each bowl with ½ tablespoon flaxseed and ⅛ cup blueberries. Serve cold.

PER SERVING   Calories: 259 | Fat: 9.6 grams | Protein: 3.9 grams | Sodium: 53 milligrams | Fiber: 7.9 grams | Carbohydrates: 41.0 grams | Sugar: 24.8 grams

POWER SOURCES

BANANA: potassium and magnesium support motor control activities in the central nervous system

BLUEBERRIES: anthocyanins prevent degeneration within the brain

FLAXSEED: omega-3s improve cholesterol levels

Dirty Rice with Beans, Peppers, and Spinach

Prep Time: 10 minutes | **Cook Time:** 10 minutes | **Serves 2**

1 tablespoon olive oil

½ small red bell pepper, seeded and chopped

½ small green bell pepper, seeded and chopped

1 small yellow onion, peeled and chopped

1 small tomato, chopped

1 (8-ounce) can black beans, rinsed and drained

2 cups spinach

1 teaspoon salt

1 teaspoon pepper

¼ teaspoon cayenne

2 cups cooked brown rice

POWER SOURCES

RICE: fiber cleanses the colon and improves nutrient absorption of essential vitamins and minerals

BLACK BEANS: protein provides support to the enzymatic reactions that produce energy

TOMATO: potassium supports nerve cell health and communication in the brain and body

BELL PEPPER: antioxidants protect organs and cells on which the brain relies on for support

1 In a skillet over medium heat, drizzle olive oil and add peppers and onions. Cook for 5–7 minutes, stirring consistently until fork-tender.

2 Add tomatoes and beans to skillet and cook for 1 minute or until cooked through. Remove from heat and stir in spinach until leaves are wilted. Season with salt, pepper, and cayenne and stir to combine well.

3 Place 1 cup rice in each of two serving bowls and top each with equal amounts of the tomato-bean mixture. Serve warm.

PER SERVING   Calories: 395 | Fat: 8.3 grams | Protein: 13.0 grams | Sodium: 1308 milligrams | Fiber: 12.5 grams | Carbohydrates: 68.0 grams | Sugar: 5.0 grams

❋ POWER BOWL PRIORITIES

While it may seem like the color is the only difference between brown and white rice, their differing nutritional content also sets them apart. During the process of turning long-grain brown rice to white, the rice loses 80 percent of its B_1, 67 percent of its B_3, 90 percent of it's B_6, 50 percent of its manganese and phosphorous, 60 percent of its iron, and 100 percent of its fiber and essential fatty acids. So when you prepare to pack your power bowls with delicious and nutritious rice, always opt for the rich, beneficial brown variety.

CHAPTER 8
Bowls for Heart Health

Strokes, heart attacks, and cardiac arrest can be terrifying, life-altering, and even fatal conditions. And the surprising aspect of heart disease is that the majority of risk factors that contribute to the development of the disease can be traced not only to genetics but to lifestyle choices like smoking, excessive alcohol consumption, inactivity, and poor dietary habits. The good news is that with a heart-healthy diet made up of the power bowl recipes found in this chapter, the risks of developing heart disease can be minimized successfully.

These heart-healthy recipes are packed with omega-rich foods that help cleanse the blood of harmful plaque, fiber that reduces cholesterol, fruits and vegetables that provide an abundance of heart-healthy vitamins and minerals, and spices and other additions that fight inflammation. With each ingredient providing benefits to the body, brain, and all of the intricate systems that work to make every day one to enjoy, these power bowls make living healthy (and eating for a healthier heart!) a simple, easy, and delicious routine that's not just a diet but a better way of life!

Oats and Berries Bowl

Prep Time: 5 minutes | **Cook Time:** N/A | **Serves 2**

1 cup nonfat Greek yogurt

1 tablespoon honey

1 cup prepared quick-cooking oats

2 tablespoons blueberries

2 tablespoons sliced strawberries, tops removed

1 tablespoon ground flaxseed

1 In a large bowl, combine yogurt and honey and stir to combine.

2 Place ½ cup prepared oats in each of two serving bowls; top each with half the yogurt mixture, 1 tablespoon blueberries, 1 tablespoon strawberries, and ½ tablespoon flaxseed. Serve chilled.

PER SERVING Calories: 209 | Fat: 3.0 grams | Protein: 15.5 grams | Sodium: 53 milligrams | Fiber: 3.5 grams | Carbohydrates: 30.8 grams | Sugar: 15.2 grams

POWER SOURCES

OATS: fiber helps regulate blood sugar

BLUEBERRIES: anthocyanins help dilate and clear blood vessels

STRAWBERRIES: vitamin C supports blood health with antioxidant benefits

FLAXSEED: omega-3s and -6s strengthen heartbeats for reduced incidence of arrhythmia

Lemon-Berry Smoothie with Turmeric

Prep Time: 5 minutes | **Cook Time:** N/A | **Serves 2**

1 lemon, peeled, seeded, and quartered

1 cup plus 1 tablespoon blueberries, divided

1 cup strawberries, tops removed, plus 2 strawberries, tops removed and sliced, divided

1 teaspoon honey

1 teaspoon ground turmeric

2 cups nonfat plain yogurt

½ cup unsweetened almond milk

1 cup ice

1 In a large blender, combine lemon, 1 cup blueberries, 1 cup strawberries, honey, and turmeric and blend on high until berries are broken down, about 1–2 minutes.

2 Add yogurt and almond milk and blend on high until thoroughly combined.

3 Add ice gradually while blending on high and blend until smooth.

4 Pour equal amounts of smoothie into each of two serving bowls; top each bowl with ½ tablespoon blueberries and 1 sliced strawberry. Serve chilled.

PER SERVING Calories: 222 | Fat: 1.4 grams | Protein: 15.8 grams | Sodium: 230 milligrams | Fiber: 4.4 grams | Carbohydrates: 38.8 grams | Sugar: 30.5 grams

POWER SOURCES

LEMON: vitamin C improves immunity

BLUEBERRIES: anthocyanins reduce new plaque formation in the bloodstream and arteries for reduced incidence of heart attack

TURMERIC: anti-inflammatory benefits increase vessel dilation for improved blood flow to and from the heart

Two-Toned Gazpacho with Quinoa

Prep Time: 10 minutes | **Cook Time:** N/A | **Serves 2**

3 small red tomatoes, chopped

3 small yellow tomatoes, chopped

1 small yellow onion, peeled and chopped

1 clove garlic

1 cup cooked quinoa

½ cup plus 2 tablespoons chopped fresh cilantro, divided

1 teaspoon salt

1 In a large blender, combine tomatoes, onions, and garlic and blend on high until all ingredients are thoroughly blended.

2 In a large bowl, pour tomato mixture and fold in quinoa and ½ cup cilantro; season with salt.

3 Pour equal amounts of gazpacho into each of two serving bowls and garnish each with 1 tablespoon cilantro. Serve chilled.

PER SERVING   Calories: 197 | Fat: 2.4 grams | Protein: 8.9 grams | Sodium: 1250 milligrams | Fiber: 7.1 grams | Carbohydrates: 38.0 grams | Sugar: 5.8 grams

POWER SOURCES

RED TOMATO: beta carotene provides protection against free-radical damage

YELLOW TOMATO: potassium supports normal functioning of cardiac muscle

CILANTRO: polyphenols act to improve immune system functioning

QUINOA: amino acids provide support to the processes of energy production

Spinach Salad with Pomegranate, Citrus, and Tofu-Avocado Cream

Prep Time: 10 minutes | **Cook Time:** N/A | **Serves 2**

- 1 small avocado, halved, pitted, and peeled
- 4 ounces silken tofu
- 2 tablespoons balsamic vinegar
- 2 tablespoons olive oil, divided
- 4 cups spinach
- 1 small grapefruit, peeled, seeded, and sliced
- 1 small orange, peeled, seeded, and sliced
- 1 cup pomegranate jewels

1 In a large blender, combine avocado, tofu, balsamic vinegar, and 1 tablespoon olive oil. Blend on high until all ingredients are combined. Drizzle in remaining 1 tablespoon olive oil while blending on high until creamy consistency develops.

2 In a large bowl, combine spinach and avocado-tofu dressing and toss to coat.

3 Pour equal amounts of salad into each of two serving bowls; top each with half the grapefruit and orange and ½ cup pomegranate. Serve chilled.

PER SERVING Calories: 512 | Fat: 27.6 grams | Protein: 15.5 grams | Sodium: 65 milligrams | Fiber: 14.4 grams | Carbohydrates: 54.5 grams | Sugar: 36.0 grams

POWER SOURCES

SPINACH: iron improves oxygen transport capability of the blood

POMEGRANATE: polyphenols provide protection against atherosclerosis

AVOCADO: potassium helps manage blood pressure

Mediterranean Salmon and Vegetables with Rice

Prep Time: 5 minutes | **Cook Time:** 20 minutes | **Serves 2**

1 tablespoon olive oil

2 (6-ounce) salmon fillets

1 cup halved green beans

1 cup cherry tomatoes

1 cup quartered raw artichokes

1 cup pitted and halved olives

2 tablespoons lemon juice

2 cups cooked wild rice

POWER SOURCES

SALMON: omega-3s provide protection against ischemic stroke

TOMATO: vitamin C promotes fast healing of injuries

OLIVE OIL: monounsaturated fats stabilize cholesterol levels

RICE: fiber contributes to the reduced incidence of type 2 diabetes development through better regulated blood sugar levels

1 Preheat oven to 375°F and grease a 13" × 9" pan with 1 tablespoon olive oil.

2 Place salmon fillets in pan and scatter beans, tomatoes, artichokes, and olives around fillets. Drizzle with lemon juice and bake for 15–20 minutes or until fish is flaky and cooked through. Remove from heat.

3 Place 1 cup rice in each of two serving bowls. Top each bowl with equal amounts of vegetable mixture and 1 salmon fillet. Serve hot.

PER SERVING   Calories: 655 | Fat: 16.4 grams | Protein: 51.6 grams | Sodium: 710 milligrams | Fiber: 18.7 grams | Carbohydrates: 72.9 grams | Sugar: 4.3 grams

Slow-Cooker Ginger Chicken with Curried Vegetables

Prep Time: 10 minutes | **Cook Time:** 4 hours | **Serves 2**

2 medium potatoes, cut into ½" cubes

1 (4-ounce) chicken breast, cut into ½" cubes

2 medium carrots, peeled and sliced, plus ¼ cup peeled and shredded carrots, divided

2 celery stalks, sliced

1 large tomato, sliced

1 small yellow onion, peeled and sliced

1 tablespoon olive oil

1 garlic clove, minced

1" gingerroot, peeled and minced

1 teaspoon curry powder

1 teaspoon salt

1 Place potatoes, chicken, sliced carrots, celery, tomato, and onion in a slow cooker.

2 Drizzle with olive oil and add garlic, ginger, curry, and salt. Stir to combine.

3 Set slow cooker on high for 4 hours.

4 Pour equal amounts of curry mixture into each of two serving bowls. Garnish each with ⅛ cup shredded carrots. Serve hot.

PER SERVING   Calories: 393 | Fat: 8.0 grams | Protein: 19.4 grams | Sodium: 1300 milligrams | Fiber: 12.1 grams | Carbohydrates: 62.6 grams | Sugar: 11.3 grams

POWER SOURCES

CARROT: vitamin A promotes healing and illness prevention

CELERY: sodium and potassium maintain and support nerve cell health

POTATO: carbohydrate source for necessary energy production

Chocolate-Banana Smoothie with Nuts and Flaxseed

Prep Time: 10 minutes | **Cook Time:** N/A | **Serves 2**

3 ounces dark chocolate

3 cups sweetened almond milk

1 medium banana, peeled and sliced, divided

2 tablespoons flaxseed

1 cup ice

½ cup shelled and crushed walnuts

POWER SOURCES

DARK CHOCOLATE: polyphenols improve blood clotting and blood vessel constriction in the heart to reduce blocked arteries

BANANA: potassium supports cognitive functioning

FLAXSEED: fiber cleanses the colon for improved nutrient absorption

1 In a large blender, combine chocolate and almond milk and blend on high until emulsified, about 2 minutes.

2 Add half the banana slices to blender and blend on high until well combined, about 1 minute.

3 Add flaxseed and blend on high until all ingredients are emulsified and thoroughly combined.

4 Add ice gradually while blending on high and blend until smooth.

5 Pour half the smoothie mixture into each of two serving bowls, then garnish each bowl with ⅛ cup walnuts and half the remaining banana slices. Serve cold.

PER SERVING   Calories: 634 | Fat: 41.0 grams | Protein: 11.1 grams | Sodium: 248 milligrams | Fiber: 9.7 grams | Carbohydrates: 54.8 grams | Sugar: 34.3 grams

Tempeh Cucumber Salad with Dill-Yogurt Sauce

Prep Time: 10 minutes | **Cook Time:** 10 minutes | **Serves 2**

1 tablespoon olive oil

8 ounces tempeh, sliced lengthwise into patties

3 tablespoons honey, divided

1 cup nonfat plain yogurt

¼ cup chopped dill

2 tablespoons red wine vinegar

2 cups chopped spinach

1 small cucumber, peeled and chopped

2 cups chopped kale

1 cup cooked quinoa

1 Coat a large skillet with olive oil and heat over medium heat. Add tempeh and cook for 5 minutes or until golden brown. Flip tempeh, drizzle with 1 tablespoon honey, and cook for 5 minutes or until golden brown. Remove from heat.

2 In a large bowl whisk together yogurt, dill, vinegar, and 2 tablespoons honey. Add spinach, cucumber, and kale and toss until coated.

3 Place ½ cup quinoa in each of two serving bowls. Then layer each with half the salad and half the tempeh. Serve warm or chilled.

PER SERVING   Calories: 604 | Fat: 18.7 grams | Protein: 36.4 grams | Sodium: 144 milligrams | Fiber: 7.2 grams | Carbohydrates: 76.8 grams | Sugar: 37.3 grams

POWER SOURCES

KALE: omega-3s and -6s prevent the formation of new plaque in the bloodstream

YOGURT: calcium supports healthy communication between the nervous and cardiovascular systems

HONEY: natural antioxidants support cell health while removing free radicals from blood and tissue

Chilled Sweet Spiced Squash Soup

Prep Time: 10 minutes | **Cook Time:** 30 minutes | **Serves 2**

1 small sweet potato, peeled and cut into 1" cubes

1 small acorn squash, peeled, seeded, and cut into 1" cubes

4 cups water

1" gingerroot, peeled and minced

1 cup spinach

2 cups plus 2 tablespoons nonfat yogurt, divided

1 cup unsweetened almond milk

2 teaspoons ground nutmeg

1 Place sweet potato and squash cubes in a stockpot. Cover with 4 cups water and bring to a boil over high heat. Once boiling, reduce heat to a simmer. Add ginger and boil for 20 minutes or until fork-tender. Remove from heat and drain.

2 Add spinach and stir until leaves are wilted. Allow to cool for 10 minutes.

3 Add 2 cups yogurt to pot and use an immersion blender on high to blend ingredients until thoroughly combined.

4 Add almond milk gradually while blending on high until desired consistency is achieved.

5 Pour equal amounts of soup into each of two serving bowls; top each with 1 tablespoon yogurt and 1 teaspoon nutmeg. Serve warm or chilled.

PER SERVING   Calories: 278 | Fat: 2.5 grams | Protein: 18.1 grams | Sodium: 326 milligrams | Fiber: 4.4 grams | Carbohydrates: 47.4 grams | Sugar: 22.6 grams

POWER SOURCES

SPINACH: vitamin A supports cell growth

YOGURT: probiotics promote gut health and improve immune system functioning

ACORN SQUASH: fiber helps lower unhealthy blood cholesterol levels

SWEET POTATO: low-glycemic complex carbohydrates help to maintain steady blood sugar levels

☀ POWER BOWL PRIORITIES

If you find yourself prepping your favorite recipe, but are out of almond milk, you can use some simple ingredients you probably already have on hand to make a fresh at-home alternative that's super nutritious and delicious! Simply combine 2 cups of natural almonds with 2 cups of purified water in a large blender and blend on high until almonds are fully broken down, and you'll have fresh almond milk that can be stored in an air-tight container in the fridge for 5–7 days . . . if it lasts that long!

Creamy Salmon Salad with Avocado "Mayo"

Prep Time: 10 minutes | **Cook Time:** 20 minutes | **Serves 2**

2 (6-ounce) salmon fillets

1 tablespoon olive oil

1 teaspoon salt

2 small avocados, peeled and pitted

½ cup nonfat plain yogurt

2 tablespoons honey

4 cups kale

1 stalk celery, chopped

1 small apple, peeled, cored, and chopped

1 Preheat oven to 375°F; set salmon fillets in a glass pan and coat with olive oil. Season with salt and bake for 20 minutes or until cooked through and flaky. Remove from oven and set aside to cool.

2 In a large blender, combine avocados, yogurt, and honey and blend on high until all ingredients are thoroughly combined, about 3–5 minutes.

3 In a large bowl, shred salmon into flakes. Add avocado mixture to salmon mixture and toss to coat.

4 Place 2 cups kale in each of two serving bowls, top each bowl with half the salmon mixture, and garnish each with half the celery and apples. Serve chilled.

PER SERVING   Calories: 635 | Fat: 28.9 grams | Protein: 42.8 grams | Sodium: 1375 milligrams | Fiber: 11.6 grams | Carbohydrates: 45.3 grams | Sugar: 29.8 grams

POWER SOURCES

SALMON: protein improves energy

KALE: vitamin A acts as an antioxidant

APPLE: fiber supports blood health and digestive health

Caprese Tempeh with Rice Noodles

Prep Time: 10 minutes | **Cook Time:** 5 minutes | **Serves 2**

4 cups water

1 (8-ounce) package rice noodles

¼ cup olive oil

1 cup chopped fresh basil, divided

8 ounces cubed tempeh

4 ounces chopped part-skim
   mozzarella cheese

4 small tomatoes, chopped

1 teaspoon salt

1 Bring a pot of with 4 cups water to a boil over high heat. Add rice noodles, reduce to a simmer, and cook until al dente, about 5 minutes.

2 Remove noodles from heat and drain.

3 In a large bowl, combine rice noodles, olive oil, and ½ cup basil leaves and stir to combine.

4 Add cubed tempeh, mozzarella, and tomatoes to noodles and toss to combine.

5 Layer equal amounts of the rice noodle mixture in each of two serving bowls, season each bowl with ½ teaspoon salt, and top each with ¼ cup basil. Serve warm or cold.

PER SERVING   Calories: 1075 | Fat: 47.2 grams | Protein: 43.7 grams | Sodium: 1774 milligrams | Fiber: 4.2 grams | Carbohydrates: 112.6 grams | Sugar: 6.2 grams

POWER SOURCES

TOMATO: magnesium promotes healthy cardiovascular system functioning and regulates heartbeat for reduced incidence of arrhythmia

BASIL: antioxidants protect red and white blood cells from oxidative stress

OLIVE OIL: monounsaturated fats reduce LDL levels in the blood

CHAPTER 9

Bowls to Regulate Blood Sugar

The prevalence of blood-sugar-related conditions such as hypoglycemia, hyperglycemia, and type 2 diabetes is increasing among Americans at a shocking rate every year. In fact, the American Diabetes Association estimates that 9.3 percent of the population suffers from type 2 diabetes, and their recommendations for avoiding the disease and its associated conditions place a large focus on a healthy diet.

The power bowls found in this chapter are perfect for anyone struggling with blood-sugar issues, because they focus on whole foods that provide the body with clean sources of carbohydrates, proteins, and healthy fats. These power bowl recipes also include low glycemic-index (GI) foods such as complex carbohydrates like fruits, vegetables, and whole grains that help to satisfy hunger while maintaining steady blood sugar levels. So whip up some power-packed power bowls, keep your blood sugar in check, and minimize the risks associated with blood-sugar-related illnesses and diseases over time.

Sesame Chicken and Vegetable Lettuce Wraps

Prep Time: 5 minutes | **Cook Time:** 10 minutes | **Serves 2**

1 tablespoon olive oil

1 small yellow onion, peeled and chopped

½ small red bell pepper, seeded and chopped

1 tablespoon sesame oil

1 small zucchini, ends removed and sliced

1 (4-ounce) chicken breast, cut into 8 (¼"-wide) strips

1 teaspoon salt

1 teaspoon garlic powder

1 tablespoon sesame seeds

4 Bibb lettuce leaves

1 Coat a large skillet with olive oil and heat over medium heat. Add onions and peppers and cook for 4–5 minutes or until opaque.

2 Add sesame oil, zucchini, and chicken strips and cook until chicken is cooked through, about 5 minutes. Remove from heat.

3 Season with salt and garlic powder and sprinkle with sesame seeds.

4 Place 2 lettuce leaves in each of two serving bowls and pour equal amounts of chicken and vegetable mixture into each. Serve hot.

PER SERVING   Calories: 224 | Fat: 14.5 grams | Protein: 14.7 grams | Sodium: 1170 milligrams | Fiber: 2.4 grams | Carbohydrates: 8.3 grams | Sugar: 3.6 grams

POWER SOURCES

CHICKEN: vitamin B_{12} supports red blood cell production

BELL PEPPER: vitamin C promotes healthy immune system protection

LETTUCE: fiber helps regulate blood sugar levels

☀ POWER BOWL PRIORITIES

In recent decades, farmers have introduced growth hormones (such as rBGH) and antibiotics to their herds. While the meat density and milk production of these animals increased profits, the quality of the products was questionable. The inorganic products farmed from hormone- and antibiotic-rich cows, pigs, and chickens were thought to contribute to accelerated maturity in human consumers. Inorganic products have also been tied to a number of health conditions such as allergies, skin issues, and systemic complications caused by antibiotic-resistant bacteria. In order to reap the maximum benefits from your power bowls, opt for meats and meat products that are antibiotic- and hormone-free.

Winter Vegetable Bisque

Prep Time: 10 minutes | **Cook Time:** 20 minutes | **Serves 2**

2 tablespoons olive oil

1 small zucchini, chopped

1 small yellow squash, chopped

2 medium carrots, peeled and chopped

1 small yellow onion, peeled and chopped

1 garlic clove, minced

5 cups unsweetened almond milk

4 small tomatoes, chopped, divided

1 teaspoon salt

1 teaspoon pepper

1 cup cooked barley

1 In a large pot over medium-high heat, drizzle olive oil and add zucchini, squash, carrots, onion, and garlic. Cook for 5 minutes or until slightly tender, then add almond milk. Bring to a boil, reduce heat to simmer, add all tomatoes except 2 tablespoons, and stir to combine thoroughly; simmer for 15 minutes or until vegetables are fork-tender. Remove from heat.

2 Season with salt and pepper and use an immersion blender to blend on high for 2–4 minutes or until all ingredients are emulsified.

3 Add barley to pot and stir to combine.

4 Pour equal amounts of bisque into each of two serving bowls. Top each bowl with 1 tablespoon reserved chopped tomato. Serve hot or cold.

PER SERVING   Calories: 382 | Fat: 20.2 grams | Protein: 8.5 grams | Sodium: 1622 milligrams | Fiber: 9.0 grams | Carbohydrates: 43.4 grams | Sugar: 12.1 grams

POWER SOURCES

ZUCCHINI: magnesium promotes healthy heartbeat regularity

BARLEY: fiber helps maintain steady blood sugar levels

CARROT: beta carotene provides antioxidant protection against free-radical damage

TOMATO: lycopene acts as an antioxidant for cell health protection

OLIVE OIL: healthy fats promote a healthy cholesterol balance

Apple-Cinnamon Oats with Tofu Cream

Prep Time: 5 minutes | **Cook Time:** 5 minutes | **Serves 2**

2 cups cooked rolled oats

2 small apples, peeled, cored, and chopped

1 teaspoon cinnamon

4 ounces chopped silken tofu

1 teaspoon honey

1 Prepare oats as directed. Remove from heat and stir in apple and cinnamon.

2 In a blender, combine tofu and honey and blend on high until well blended and creamy, about 1–2 minutes.

3 Layer equal amounts of oats and apples in each of two serving bowls and top each with equal amounts of tofu cream.

4 Serve hot or chilled.

PER SERVING   Calories: 324 | Fat: 7.7 grams | Protein: 15.3 grams | Sodium: 16 milligrams | Fiber: 7.7 grams | Carbohydrates: 51.2 grams | Sugar: 16.8 grams

POWER SOURCES

APPLE: fiber helps regulate blood sugar

OATS: manganese contributes to proper metabolic functioning

TOFU: protein helps slow the absorption of sugar after a meal to stabilize blood sugar levels

Tomato Soup with Garbanzos and Kale

Prep Time: 10 minutes | **Cook Time:** 25 minutes | **Serves 2**

1 tablespoon olive oil

1 small yellow onion, peeled and chopped

1 clove garlic

8 small tomatoes, crushed

2 kale leaves, chopped

4 cups water

1 teaspoon salt

1 teaspoon pepper

1 (8-ounce) can garbanzo beans, rinsed and drained

POWER SOURCES

TOMATO: vitamin A fights free-radical damage in cells

GARBANZO BEANS: fiber regulates blood sugar levels

OLIVE OIL: healthy fats promote healthy cholesterol levels in the bloodstream

1 In a large pot over medium-high heat, drizzle olive oil and add onions and garlic, then cook for 5 minutes or until onions are opaque.

2 Add tomatoes and kale to pot and cook for 5 minutes. Add water and bring to a boil.

3 Reduce heat to low and simmer for 15 minutes. Remove from heat.

4 Season with salt and pepper and using an immersion blender blend on high until all ingredients are emulsified.

5 Add garbanzo beans and stir until thoroughly combined.

6 Pour equal amounts of soup into each of two serving bowls. Serve hot or cold.

PER SERVING   Calories: 319 | Fat: 9.2 grams | Protein: 12.8 grams | Sodium: 1451 milligrams | Fiber: 13.4 grams | Carbohydrates: 47.9 grams | Sugar: 16.2 grams

Three-Green Salad with Sweet Fruit and Nuts

Prep Time: 10 minutes | **Cook Time:** N/A | **Serves 2**

1 cup chopped kale leaves

1 cup chopped spinach leaves

1 cup chopped arugula

1 tablespoon olive oil

1 tablespoon red wine vinegar

½ small red grapefruit, peeled, seeded, and sliced

½ cup sliced strawberries, tops removed

½ cup blueberries

½ cup chopped pineapple

¼ cup shelled, crushed walnuts

1. In a large bowl, combine kale, spinach, and arugula and toss to combine.
2. Drizzle greens with olive oil and vinegar and toss to coat.
3. In a large bowl, combine grapefruit, berries, pineapple, and walnuts and toss to combine.
4. Layer equal amounts of greens in each of two serving bowls. Pour equal amounts of fruit mixture over greens. Serve chilled.

PER SERVING   Calories: 260 | Fat: 16.0 grams | Protein: 4.8 grams | Sodium: 17 milligrams | Fiber: 5.5 grams | Carbohydrates: 27.9 grams | Sugar: 19.5 grams

POWER SOURCES

KALE: fiber helps to regulate blood sugar levels

SPINACH: iron helps improve oxygenation in the bloodstream

ARUGULA: magnesium promotes regular heartbeat

Confetti-Quinoa Stuffed Peppers

Prep Time: 10 minutes | **Cook Time:** 30 minutes | **Serves 2**

4 large bell peppers, tops cut off and seeds and ribs removed

1 tablespoon olive oil

1 small yellow onion, peeled and chopped

1 cup corn kernels

1 garlic clove, minced

1 small tomato, chopped

½ small zucchini, chopped

1 teaspoon salt

2 cups cooked quinoa

½ cup crumbled feta

POWER SOURCES

QUINOA: omega fatty acids promote healthy fat content to stabilize blood sugar in the bloodstream

BELL PEPPER: vitamin C promotes immunity for decreased illness and disease

CORN: folate prevents cardiovascular conditions such as atherosclerosis

1 Preheat oven to 350°F.

2 Set hollowed-out peppers open-side up on a baking sheet.

3 Coat a large skillet with olive oil and heat over medium heat. Add onions, corn, and garlic and cook for 5 minutes or until opaque. Add tomato and zucchini, sprinkle with salt, and cook for 5 minutes until zucchini is tender. Remove from heat.

4 Stir quinoa into vegetable mixture and toss until thoroughly combined.

5 Spoon quinoa and veggies into peppers, compacting the mixture to the top.

6 Bake for 20 minutes or until peppers are cooked through.

7 Remove from heat, then empty the contents of 2 peppers into each of two serving bowls. Slice the peppers into strips and layer atop the quinoa. Top each bowl with ¼ cup feta. Serve hot.

PER SERVING   Calories: 537 | Fat: 18.7 grams | Protein: 19.2 grams | Sodium: 1542 milligrams | Fiber: 12.6 grams | Carbohydrates: 73.8 grams | Sugar: 20.1 grams

Super Citrus Smoothie

Prep Time: 10 minutes | **Cook Time:** N/A | **Serves 2**

½ cup water

1 lemon, peeled, seeded, and sliced

1 small pink grapefruit, peeled, seeded, and sliced

1 small orange, peeled, seeded, and sliced

1 cup plus 2 tablespoons chopped pineapple, divided

1 cup plus 2 tablespoons nonfat yogurt, divided

1 cup ice

1. In a large blender, combine water and citrus fruits except 2 tablespoons pineapple and blend on high until all fruits are broken down and well combined, about 1–2 minutes.

2. Add 1 cup yogurt and blend on high until thoroughly combined, about 1 minute.

3. Add ice gradually while blending on high and blend until smooth.

4. Pour equal amounts of smoothie into each of two serving bowls, top each with 1 tablespoon yogurt, and garnish each with 1 tablespoon chopped pineapple. Serve cold.

PER SERVING   Calories: 235 | Fat: 0.4 grams | Protein: 10.9 grams | Sodium: 109 milligrams | Fiber: 6.0 grams | Carbohydrates: 51.7 grams | Sugar: 42.7 grams

POWER SOURCES

LEMON: limonins safeguard tissues against damage by free radicals

ORANGE: vitamin C supports immune system functioning

GRAPEFRUIT: fiber helps to promote stable blood sugar levels

YOGURT: protein helps slow the absorption of sugar after a meal to stabilize blood sugar levels

✳ POWER BOWL PRIORITIES

Vitamin C is well known for its ability to improve immunity, but this potent vitamin acts to safeguard and promote health in other ways, too. Acting as an antioxidant, vitamin C is able to prevent free-radical damage in cells for protection against illness and serious disease. Also required for more than 300 enzymatic reactions in the body, vitamin C plays a crucial role in everything from stress-reducing hormone production, metabolic functioning, and muscle maintenance to energy production and the maintenance of healthy red blood cell production.

Green Pea–Potato Soup

Prep Time: 10 minutes | **Cook Time:** 15 minutes | **Serves 2**

1 tablespoon olive oil

1 clove garlic

2 small potatoes, chopped

3 cups water

2 cups green peas

1 teaspoon salt

2 tablespoons ground flaxseed

½ cup nonfat yogurt

POWER SOURCES

PEAS: fiber helps to regulate blood sugar levels

POTATO: vitamin B_6 supports reactions that provide energy for cells

OLIVE OIL: healthy fats promote healthy blood cholesterol content

1 In a large pot over medium heat, drizzle olive oil and cook garlic for 30 seconds until fragrant.

2 Add potatoes and cover with 3 cups water. Bring to a boil, then reduce heat and simmer for 10 minutes. Remove from heat, add peas, and stir to combine.

3 Drain, reserving and returning 2 cups of water to pot. Season with salt and add flaxseed.

4 Using an immersion blender, blend ingredients on high until thoroughly blended.

5 Pour equal amounts of soup into each of two serving bowls. Dollop ¼ cup yogurt on top of each bowl; serve hot or cold.

PER SERVING Calories: 307 | Fat: 9.8 grams | Protein: 14.4 grams | Sodium: 1338 milligrams | Fiber: 12.5 grams | Carbohydrates: 41.6 grams | Sugar: 13.1 grams

Spinach and Mushroom Steak with Wild Rice

Prep Time: 10 minutes | **Cook Time:** 12 minutes | **Serves 2**

2 tablespoons olive oil, divided

1 cup sliced portobello mushrooms

8 ounces lean beef, sliced into ¼"-thick strips

1 garlic clove, minced

1 teaspoon salt

2 cups spinach

2 cups cooked wild rice

POWER SOURCES

LEAN BEEF: protein helps slow the absorption of sugar after a meal to stabilize blood sugar levels

MUSHROOMS: potassium optimizes cell health

RICE: fiber helps regulate blood sugar levels

GARLIC: allicin combats dangerous triglycerides and cholesterol levels

1. Coat a large skillet with 1 tablespoon olive oil and heat over medium heat. Add mushrooms and cook until slightly soft, about 4 minutes.

2. Add steak and garlic to mushrooms, drizzle with additional 1 tablespoon olive oil, season with salt, and cook for 5–7 minutes or until steak is cooked through and desired doneness is achieved.

3. Add spinach and stir until wilted, about 1 minute. Remove from heat.

4. Place 1 cup rice in each of two serving bowls and layer equal amounts of steak and mushroom mixture over top. Serve hot.

PER SERVING   Calories: 448 | Fat: 17.5 grams | Protein: 32.5 grams | Sodium: 1255 milligrams | Fiber: 4.2 grams | Carbohydrates: 38.2 grams | Sugar: 2.4 grams

Blue Apple Smoothie

Prep Time: 5 minutes | **Cook Time:** N/A | **Serves 2**

1 cup organic apple juice

2 cups plus 2 tablespoons blueberries, divided

1 small apple, cored

1 kale leaf, rib removed

1 cup spinach

1 cup plus 2 tablespoons nonfat yogurt, divided

1 cup ice

POWER SOURCES

APPLE: quercetin protects cells from oxidation

SPINACH: vitamin K provides immune system support

KALE: fiber helps to regulate blood sugar levels

BLUEBERRIES: anthocyanins support respiratory health

YOGURT: calcium supports mineral absorption in bones and teeth

1 In a large blender, combine apple juice, 2 cups blueberries, apple, kale, and spinach and blend on high until all ingredients are broken down and well combined, about 3–4 minutes.

2 Add 1 cup yogurt and blend on high until all ingredients are well combined, about 1–2 minutes.

3 Add ice gradually while blending on high and blend until smooth.

4 Pour equal amounts of smoothie into each of two serving bowls and top each with 1 tablespoon yogurt and 1 tablespoon blueberries. Serve cold.

PER SERVING   Calories: 256 | Fat: 0.7 grams | Protein: 10.1 grams | Sodium: 126 milligrams | Fiber: 5.3 grams | Carbohydrates: 55.8 grams | Sugar: 44.4 grams

Salmon Patties with Creamy Curry Slaw

Prep Time: 15 minutes | **Cook Time:** 15 minutes | **Serves 2**

1 (6-ounce) salmon fillet, shredded

½ cup cooked quinoa

1 teaspoon garlic powder

1 teaspoon salt

1 teaspoon ground turmeric

2 tablespoons olive oil, divided

1 cup nonfat plain yogurt

1 teaspoon curry powder

½ cup shredded red cabbage

½ cup peeled and shredded carrots

1. In a food processor, combine salmon, quinoa, garlic powder, salt, turmeric, and 1 tablespoon olive oil. Blend on high until all ingredients are broken down and thoroughly combined, about 3–5 minutes. Form mixture into 4 equal patties.

2. Coat a large skillet with the remaining 1 tablespoon olive oil and heat over medium heat. Add salmon patties and cook for 5–7 minutes on each side or until golden brown. Remove from heat.

3. In a bowl, combine yogurt, curry, and cabbage. Toss to coat.

4. Place 2 salmon patties in each of two serving bowls and top each with equal amounts of dressed slaw. Garnish each bowl with ¼ cup shredded carrots. Serve warm or chilled.

PER SERVING   Calories: 487 | Fat: 19.5 grams | Protein: 45.0 grams | Sodium: 1411 milligrams | Fiber: 3.4 grams | Carbohydrates: 25.9 grams | Sugar: 11.9 grams

POWER SOURCES

TURMERIC: anti-inflammatory agents safeguard heart against disease

SALMON: omega-3s provide antioxidant protection for cells and blood

CABBAGE: sterols block absorption of harmful dietary cholesterols

YOGURT: protein helps slow the absorption of sugar after a meal to stabilize blood sugar levels

CHAPTER 10

Bowls for Bone Health

Supplying support for the muscles, protection for the organs, and consistent mineral and nutrient provisions for the entire body, the bones play numerous roles in safeguarding the body against harm. But did you know that they also can help improve and maintain your health as well?

Nutrient deficiencies, overuse, and illness and disease can contribute to the degradation and damage of bones over time, making them brittle and susceptible to breaks. While osteoporosis gets much of the attention in terms of dangers regarding bone health, other conditions such as osteoarthritis and osteopenia can wreak havoc on quality of life by causing aches, pains, and limitations on activity.

Fortunately, the power bowls in this chapter supply ample amounts of essential bone-building vitamins and minerals that work to strengthen bones and reduce risks to your bones' health. With rich provisions of vitamins A, Bs, C, E, and K; minerals such as calcium and magnesium; and protective antioxidants; the natural ingredients contained in these power bowl recipes ensure that your bones have exactly what they need to be strong and healthy.

Figgy Rice Pudding Bowl

Prep Time: 10 minutes | **Cook Time:** 10 minutes | **Serves 2**

½ cup organic apple juice

1½ tablespoons maple syrup, divided

5 figs (4 chopped, 1 sliced), divided

2 cups cooked white rice

1 cup nonfat Greek yogurt

2 teaspoons cinnamon

POWER SOURCES

FIGS: potassium aids in mineral absorption for proper calcium maintenance

YOGURT: calcium supports bone strength

CINNAMON: antimicrobial compounds reduce incidences of illness

1 In a small pot over medium-high heat, combine apple juice, 1 tablespoon maple syrup, and chopped figs and cook until slightly reduced and thickened, about 7–10 minutes. Remove from heat.

2 Stir rice into fig mixture and toss to coat.

3 In a small bowl, combine yogurt, remaining ½ tablespoon maple syrup, and cinnamon and whisk to combine.

4 Pour equal amounts of fig mixture into each of two serving bowls and top each with equal amounts of cinnamon yogurt.

5 Top each bowl with half the sliced figs. Serve chilled.

PER SERVING   Calories: 436 | Fat: 0.7 grams | Protein: 16.9 grams | Sodium: 53 milligrams | Fiber: 5.8 grams | Carbohydrates: 92.1 grams | Sugar: 40.0 grams

❋ POWER BOWL PRIORITIES

While calcium-packed dairy choices like milk and other dairy products are often considered great sources of the essential bone-building mineral, surprising sources like greens, spinach, and broccoli can also provide your bones with an abundance of calcium, zinc, and protein.

Creamy Chicken and Rice Bowl

Prep Time: 10 minutes | **Cook Time:** 10 minutes | **Serves 2**

2 tablespoons olive oil

1 cup peeled and chopped carrots

2 (4-ounce) chicken breasts, cut into 1" cubes

½ cup low-sodium chicken broth

1 cup peas

1 teaspoon salt

1 teaspoon garlic powder

1 cup nonfat Greek yogurt

2 cups cooked wild rice

1 Coat a large skillet with olive oil and heat over medium heat. Add carrots and cook for 5 minutes or until slightly softened.

2 Add chicken, broth, and peas and season with salt and garlic powder. Cook for 5–7 minutes or until chicken is cooked through and juices run clear. Remove from heat.

3 Add yogurt to chicken mixture and stir until all ingredients are coated and thoroughly combined.

4 Pour 1 cup rice into each of two serving bowls and top each with equal amounts of chicken mixture. Serve hot.

PER SERVING   Calories: 566 | Fat: 15.4 grams | Protein: 47.9 grams | Sodium: 1455 milligrams | Fiber: 9.3 grams | Carbohydrates: 58.4 grams | Sugar: 12.6 grams

POWER SOURCES

CARROT: vitamin A acts as an antioxidant to protect against cancerous cellular changes

RICE: selenium supports enzymatic reactions in metabolic processes

YOGURT: calcium contributes to necessary mineral storage in bones and teeth

Pecan Pie Smoothie Bowl

Prep Time: 5 minutes | **Cook Time:** N/A | **Serves 2**

2 cups almond milk

2 dates, pitted

1 cup plus 2 tablespoons shelled pecans, divided

¼ cup plus 2 tablespoons cashews, divided

1 teaspoon maple syrup

1 cup nonfat yogurt

1 cup ice

POWER SOURCES

PECANS: omega-3s protect against free-radical damage

YOGURT: calcium improves strength and density of bones

DATES: potassium helps regulate blood pressure

CASHEWS: monounsaturated fats help protect against heart disease

1 In a large blender, combine almond milk and dates and blend on high until dates are emulsified, about 1–2 minutes.

2 Add 1 cup pecans and ¼ cup cashews to blender and blend on high until nuts are broken down and thoroughly combined, about 1–2 minutes.

3 Add syrup and yogurt and blend on high until all ingredients are thoroughly combined, about 1 minute.

4 Add ice gradually while blending on high and blend until smooth.

5 Pour equal amounts of smoothie into each of two serving bowls and top each with 1 tablespoon pecans and 1 tablespoon cashews. Serve chilled.

PER SERVING   Calories: 743 | Fat: 53.1 grams | Protein: 17.6 grams | Sodium: 257 milligrams | Fiber: 7.8 grams | Carbohydrates: 53.9 grams | Sugar: 37.9 grams

Rosemary Pesto Chicken and Broccoli Bowl

Prep Time: 10 minutes | **Cook Time:** 25 minutes | **Serves 2**

4 cups water

2 cups bowtie pasta

2 cups steamed broccoli florets

2 tablespoons plus ¼ cup olive oil, divided

2 (4-ounce) chicken breasts, halved lengthwise

2 teaspoons salt

2 garlic cloves

¼ cup rosemary

¼ cup shredded Parmesan cheese

POWER SOURCES

OLIVE OIL: healthy fats promote healthy blood cholesterol

CHICKEN: protein and B vitamins ensure optimal muscle and blood health

BROCCOLI: vitamin K helps synthesize a bone protein called osteocalcin that helps to create bones

PARMESAN CHEESE: amino acids support healthy enzymatic reactions in metabolic processes

1   In a large pot over high heat, bring 4 cups water to a boil, add pasta, and cook 10 minutes or until al dente. Strain. Toss broccoli florets with pasta until thoroughly combined. Remove from heat and set aside.

2   Coat a large skillet with 2 tablespoons olive oil and heat over medium heat. Add chicken breast halves and cook for 5–7 minutes or until golden. Flip breasts, season with salt, and cook for additional 7 minutes until cooked through and juices run clear.

3   In a large blender, combine ¼ cup olive oil, garlic, rosemary, and Parmesan cheese and blend on high until all ingredients are broken down and fully combined.

4   Layer equal amounts of pasta and broccoli in each of two serving bowls. Place 2 chicken breast halves on top of each bowl and spoon equal amounts of pesto over chicken. Serve hot.

PER SERVING   Calories: 725 | Fat: 38.9 grams | Protein: 38.0 grams | Sodium: 2528 milligrams | Fiber: 7.2 grams | Carbohydrates: 53.6 grams | Sugar: 3.7 grams

Mojo Chicken, Black Beans, and Rice Bowl

Prep Time: 5 minutes | **Cook Time:** 10 minutes | **Serves 2**

2 (4-ounce) chicken breasts, cut into ½"-thick strips

1 cup orange juice

½ cup chicken broth

¼ cup chopped fresh oregano

2 teaspoons black pepper

2 cups canned, rinsed, and drained black beans

1 teaspoon salt

2 cups cooked wild rice

1 In a large skillet over medium heat, combine chicken, orange juice, chicken broth, oregano, and pepper and cook until chicken is cooked through, about 10 minutes.

2 Stir black beans into chicken mixture, season with salt, and toss to combine thoroughly. Remove from heat.

3 Layer equal amounts of rice into each of two serving bowls, then top with equal amounts of chicken mixture. Serve hot.

PER SERVING   Calories: 598 | Fat: 2.6 grams | Protein: 50.3 grams | Sodium: 1715 milligrams | Fiber: 25.6 grams | Carbohydrates: 95.1 grams | Sugar: 16.3 grams

POWER SOURCES

CITRUS: vitamin C supports the immune system to prevent illness and disease

BLACK BEANS: fiber promotes healthy mineral absorption and distribution in the bloodstream

CHICKEN: protein supports the consistent maintenance of energy levels

RICE: manganese provides specific enzymes that play a role in the formation of bones

Creamy Coriander Cabbage and Carrot Soup

Prep Time: 15 minutes | **Cook Time:** 30 minutes | **Serves 2**

- 4 cups unsweetened vanilla almond milk
- 1 tablespoon ground coriander
- 4 celery stalks (2 chopped, 2 whole), divided
- 2 cups chopped green cabbage
- 5 medium carrots, peeled and chopped
- 2 teaspoons salt
- 1 teaspoon pepper
- 1 cup nonfat Greek yogurt

POWER SOURCES

ALMOND MILK: vitamin E acts as an antioxidant to protect the body from damaging free radicals

CABBAGE: sterols support healthy blood cholesterol levels

GREEK YOGURT: calcium strengthens bones

1. In a large stockpot over high heat, combine almond milk, coriander, chopped celery, cabbage, and carrots. Bring to a boil, reduce heat to simmer, and cook for 20 minutes or until all ingredients are softened. Remove from heat and cool for 10 minutes.

2. Using an immersion blender, blend ingredients on high until broken down and thoroughly combined, about 1–2 minutes.

3. Season with salt and pepper and stir in yogurt. Blend on high until all ingredients are well blended.

4. Pour equal amounts of soup into each of two serving bowls. Garnish each bowl with 1 whole celery stalk. Serve hot or cold.

PER SERVING   Calories: 223 | Fat: 5.8 grams | Protein: 16.6 grams | Sodium: 2874 milligrams | Fiber: 8.2 grams | Carbohydrates: 26.6 grams | Sugar: 12.8 grams

❋ POWER BOWL PRIORITIES

Multiple studies have shown the dramatic difference between the benefits of diets that include regular consumption of oats versus those void of oats. These delicious grains not only promote satiety and improve energy levels, but they also protect heart health. By protecting healthy blood cholesterol, reducing harmful cholesterol, regulating blood sugar, and maintaining healthy blood pressure, the fiber from oats also helps to combat atherosclerosis and plaque buildup within arteries. So if you're eating for heart health, include at least six ¼-cup servings per week for maximum benefits.

Thai Steak Stir-Fry

Prep Time: 10 minutes | **Cook Time:** 15 minutes | **Serves 2**

2 tablespoons sesame oil, divided

1 cup peeled and sliced carrots

1 cup chopped lemongrass

2 tablespoons low-sodium soy
sauce

12 ounces lean beef, sliced into
¼" strips

1 cup pea pods

1 tablespoon curry powder

1 teaspoon garlic powder

2 cups cooked rice noodles

½ cup peeled and shredded
carrots

1 Coat a large skillet with 1 tablespoon sesame oil and
heat over medium heat. Add carrots and lemongrass
and cook until slightly softened, about 7 minutes.

2 Drizzle 1 tablespoon sesame oil and soy sauce in skillet
and add beef and pea pods. Season with curry powder
and garlic powder and stir while cooking for 5–7 minutes or until beef is cooked through.

3 Add rice noodles to skillet and toss to combine ingredients thoroughly. Remove from heat.

4 Pour equal amounts of noodles into each of two serving bowls.

5 Pour equal amounts of stir-fry over noodles. Garnish
each with ¼ cup shredded carrots. Serve hot.

PER SERVING   Calories: 680 | Fat: 24.4 grams | Protein:
43.6 grams | Sodium: 703 milligrams | Fiber:
7.1 grams | Carbohydrates: 65.6 grams | Sugar: 5.9 grams

POWER SOURCES

LEAN BEEF: B vitamins
help with healthy hormone
production and secretion

CARROT: vitamin A combats
free-radical damage

PEA PODS: manganese may
promote bone health

Apple Crumble with Cinnamon Cream

Prep Time: 10 minutes | **Cook Time:** 30 minutes | **Serves 2**

4 small apples, cored and sliced into ½" slices

¼ cup organic apple juice

1 cup rolled oats

1 tablespoon maple syrup

2 teaspoons cinnamon, divided

1 cup nonfat yogurt

POWER SOURCES

APPLE: quercetin combats free-radical damage

OATS: zinc supports the immune system's functioning

YOGURT: calcium strengthens bones and teeth

CINNAMON: manganese promotes proper blood clotting

1 Preheat oven to 375°F.

2 Place apple slices in a 9" × 9" glass dish. Pour apple juice over apples and bake for 15 minutes or until softened.

3 In a medium bowl, combine oats and maple syrup with 1 teaspoon cinnamon. Sprinkle mixture over apples and bake for 10–15 minutes or until oats are crunchy.

4 Pour equal amounts of apple and oats mixture into each of two serving bowls. Top each bowl with ½ cup yogurt and ½ teaspoon cinnamon. Serve hot or cold.

PER SERVING   Calories: 422 | Fat: 2.6 grams | Protein: 12.3 grams | Sodium: 100 milligrams | Fiber: 12.7 grams | Carbohydrates: 90.3 grams | Sugar: 50.0 grams

Ginger-Fennel-Tofu Soup with Red Lentils and Barley

Prep Time: 5 minutes | **Cook Time:** 15 minutes | **Serves 2**

1 tablespoon olive oil

2 cups chopped fennel

1" gingerroot, peeled and chopped

1 garlic clove, chopped

12 ounces silken tofu

4 cups unsweetened almond milk

2 cups spinach

2 teaspoons salt

2 cups cooked red lentils

1 cup cooked barley

¼ cup chopped parsley

1 In a large pot over medium heat, drizzle olive oil and add fennel, ginger, and garlic. Cook until translucent, about 3–4 minutes.

2 Add tofu and almond milk and cook for 10 minutes until simmering. Add spinach and stir. Remove from heat.

3 Season with salt, then use an immersion blender on high to blend soup until all ingredients are broken down and thoroughly combined, about 2–3 minutes.

4 Stir red lentils and barley into soup until well distributed.

5 Pour equal amounts of soup into each of two serving bowls. Garnish each bowl with ⅛ cup parsley. Serve hot.

PER SERVING   Calories: 730 | Fat: 26.6 grams | Protein: 50.8 grams | Sodium: 2746 milligrams | Fiber: 26.2 grams | Carbohydrates: 77.9 grams | Sugar: 7.4 grams

POWER SOURCES

TOFU: calcium helps strengthen bones

LENTILS: phosphorus supports bone health

SPINACH: iron acts to promote oxygen delivery to muscles

Spicy Garlic Shrimp Toss

Prep Time: 5 minutes | **Cook Time:** 10 minutes | **Serves 2**

- 1 tablespoon olive oil
- 2 garlic cloves, minced
- 1 teaspoon crushed red pepper flakes
- ¼ cup lemon juice
- 1 pound shrimp, peeled and deveined
- 1 teaspoon salt
- 2 cups spinach
- 2 cups cooked rice noodles

1. Coat a large skillet with olive oil and heat over medium heat. Add garlic and cook until fragrant, about 1 minute.
2. Add pepper flakes and lemon juice to skillet and stir. Add shrimp and cook for 5–7 minutes or until pink and cooked through. Season with salt; stir in spinach until wilted. Remove from heat.
3. Place 1 cup rice noodles in each of two serving bowls and top each with half the shrimp-spinach mixture. Serve hot.

PER SERVING   Calories: 461 | Fat: 7.7 grams | Protein: 50.0 grams | Sodium: 1489 milligrams | Fiber: 2.8 grams | Carbohydrates: 47.0 grams | Sugar: 1.1 grams

POWER SOURCES

GARLIC: allicin combats dangerous triglycerides and cholesterol levels

SPINACH: vitamin K supports mineral concentration in bones and teeth for strength

LEMON: limonins act to safeguard tissues against damage by free radicals

Rice Noodles with Tofu and Roasted Squash

Prep Time: 10 minutes | **Cook Time:** 30 minutes | **Serves 2**

3 tablespoons olive oil, divided

1 small butternut squash, cut into ½" cubes

2 teaspoons salt, divided

12 ounces extra-firm tofu, sliced into 6 slices

1 teaspoon black pepper

1 teaspoon garlic powder

1 cup shelled and cooked edamame

2 cups cooked rice noodles

1 Preheat oven to 400°F and grease a baking sheet with 1 tablespoon olive oil. Scatter squash on baking sheet in an even layer, drizzle with 1 tablespoon olive oil, and season with 1 teaspoon salt. Bake for 10 minutes, turn, and continue baking for 7–10 minutes or until fork-tender with crispy exteriors. Remove from heat.

2 In a skillet over medium-high heat, drizzle 1 tablespoon olive oil and cook tofu for 5–7 minutes. Season with remaining 1 teaspoon salt, pepper, and garlic powder and flip. Cook until golden brown, about 4–5 minutes. Remove from heat and toss in edamame to thoroughly combine.

3 Place 1 cup noodles in each of two serving bowls and layer half the squash and tofu on top of each bowl. Serve hot.

PER SERVING   Calories: 575 | Fat: 22.4 grams | Protein: 29.7 grams | Sodium: 2380 milligrams | Fiber: 8.7 grams | Carbohydrates: 65.5 grams | Sugar: 4.6 grams

POWER SOURCES

TOFU: soy protein regenerates muscle tissue

OLIVE OIL: omega-3s promote healthy cardiovascular functioning

BUTTERNUT SQUASH: vitamin A combats free-radical damage in bone cells

CHAPTER 11
Bowls to Reduce Inflammation

Inflammation is the body's self-protective reaction to injury or irritation, often presenting as localized pain, heat, redness, or swelling. This condition can wreak havoc on cells, tissues, and organs throughout the body, resulting in everything from pain and arthritis to premature aging and cancers. Inflammation can also limit physical abilities, decrease quality of life, and lead to serious disease or even death.

Fortunately, certain foods that are rich in vitamins, minerals, macronutrients, and antioxidants—like the ones used in the hardworking recipes in this chapter—provide powerful protection against inflammation. And by reducing inflammation, these sweet and savory power bowls also protect cells against free-radical damage, stabilize blood sugar, increase metabolism, and slow the aging process. These benefits can help to improve your overall health and increase quality of life by bettering your quality of sleep, energy levels, brain functioning, and more! With every bite of these tasty power bowls designed to fight inflammation, you can savor the flavors of natural foods that satisfy hunger while easily achieving optimal health.

Spinach and Berry Salad with Flaxseed and Feta

Prep Time: 5 minutes | **Cook Time:** N/A | **Serves 2**

4 cups spinach

2 cups blueberries

2 cups sliced strawberries

¼ cup olive oil

2 tablespoons apple cider vinegar

1 tablespoon honey

2 tablespoons ground flaxseed

¼ cup feta cheese

1. In a large bowl, combine spinach and berries.
2. In a small bowl, whisk together oil, vinegar, honey, and flaxseed. Drizzle dressing over salad and toss to coat.
3. Pour equal amounts of salad into each of two serving bowls and top each with ⅛ cup feta.
4. Serve chilled.

PER SERVING Calories: 510 | Fat: 33.6 grams | Protein: 7.9 grams | Sodium: 224 milligrams | Fiber: 10.1 grams | Carbohydrates: 47.8 grams | Sugar: 32.6 grams

POWER SOURCES

OLIVE OIL: reduces inflammation and promotes heart health

BERRIES: anthocyanins support immunity

FLAXSEED: alpha-linolenic acid helps improve immune system functioning

APPLE CIDER VINEGAR: antimicrobial and antiviral enzymes protect against illness

POWER BOWL PRIORITIES

When you add sweet berries, crunchy greens, aromatic spices, and tasty additions that contain anti-inflammatory phytochemicals, you can ensure every power bowl you create can fight inflammation. Smoothies, salads, and every delicious entrée imaginable can boost anti-inflammatory benefits naturally and deliciously.

Pear-Berry Smoothie with Ginger

Prep Time: 5 minutes | **Cook Time:** N/A | **Serves 2**

2 cups cooled green tea

1" gingerroot, peeled and sliced

2 small pears, cored

1 cup blackberries

1 cup strawberries

1 teaspoon honey

1 cup ice

2 sprigs fresh mint

1 In a large blender, combine green tea and ginger and blend on high until ginger is broken down, about 1–2 minutes.

2 Add pears, berries, and honey to blender and blend on high until all fruits are broken down and well blended, about 2–3 minutes.

3 Add ice gradually while blending on high and blend until smooth.

4 Pour equal amounts of smoothie into each of two serving bowls. Garnish each bowl with 1 mint sprig. Serve cold.

PER SERVING   Calories: 66 | Fat: 0.4 grams | Protein: 1.5 grams | Sodium: 3 milligrams | Fiber: 5.3 grams | Carbohydrates: 16.0 grams | Sugar: 9.9 grams

POWER SOURCES

PEAR: copper combats free-radical damage

GINGER: anti-inflammatory compounds fight inflammation in tissues

GREEN TEA: rich antioxidants combat oxidation of cells

Tofu Curry with Vegetables

Prep Time: 5 minutes | **Cook Time:** 10 minutes | **Serves 2**

2 tablespoons olive oil

1 small yellow onion, peeled and chopped

½ cup minced lemongrass

1 cup chopped kale

8 ounces extra-firm tofu, cut into ¼" cubes

2 small tomatoes, chopped, divided

2 cups cooked couscous

1 teaspoon salt

2 teaspoons curry powder

1 teaspoon garlic powder

1 Coat a large skillet with olive oil and heat over medium heat. Add onion, lemongrass, kale, and tofu and cook until vegetables are fork-tender, about 5 minutes.

2 Add half the chopped tomato and couscous and sprinkle with salt, curry, and garlic. Toss to combine until heated through, about 4–5 minutes. Remove from heat.

3 Pour equal amounts of the tofu curry into each of two serving bowls. Garnish each bowl with remaining chopped tomato. Serve hot.

PER SERVING   Calories: 427 | Fat: 16.7 grams | Protein: 19.5 grams | Sodium: 27 milligrams | Fiber: 5.8 grams | Carbohydrates: 52.4 grams | Sugar: 4.7 grams

POWER SOURCES

TOFU: protein supports enzymatic reactions related to fat metabolism

CURRY: turmeric contains anti-inflammatory compounds that combat inflammation in cells and tissues

ONION: vitamin C strengthens the immune system to help the body fight germs and consequential illness and disease

KALE: vitamin A boosts immune system functioning

Two-Toned Beet Salad with Tofu and Walnuts

Prep Time: 5 minutes | **Cook Time:** 30 minutes | **Serves 2**

1 small yellow beet

1 small red beet

8 ounces silken tofu

1 tablespoon honey

1 small cucumber, peeled and chopped

2 tablespoons ground flaxseed

1 cup cooked quinoa

2 cups spinach

2 cups mixed greens

¼ cup walnuts

1. Preheat oven to 400°F, wrap the beets together in tinfoil, and roast for 20–30 minutes or until fork-tender. Remove from oven and cool.

2. Add silken tofu and honey to a blender and blend on high to combine. Pour cream into a large bowl.

3. Slice beets thinly, mix yellow and red beet slices together, then add half of beet mixture to bowl with cream. Toss to coat.

4. Add cucumber and flaxseed to bowl and toss to combine. Incorporate quinoa into salad and toss to combine throughout.

5. Layer 1 cup spinach and 1 cup greens in each of two serving bowls, then add half of the quinoa salad to each. Top each with remaining half of beets and ⅛ cup walnuts. Serve chilled.

PER SERVING   Calories: 476 | Fat: 21.6 grams | Protein: 28.3 grams | Sodium: 144 milligrams | Fiber: 12.0 grams | Carbohydrates: 48.9 grams | Sugar: 16.5 grams

POWER SOURCES

BEETS: betalain, a polyphenol in beets, protects the body from inflammation

WALNUTS: vitamin E prevents oxidative damage to cells

GREENS: iron and magnesium support mineral absorption

✳ POWER BOWL PRIORITIES

Vitamin E is an essential vitamin for all of the processes throughout the body. Whether you've suffered a burn, come into contact with toxic air pollutants, or experienced any number of illnesses or diseases that are caused by free-radical damage, vitamin E possesses the healing powers to help. Offering protection for everything from the bones and the brain to the skin, heart, and lungs, vitamin E is one multitasking nutrient you should be sure you're getting enough of in your diet.

Beet and Cashew Hummus with Vegetables and Quinoa

Prep Time: 10 minutes | **Cook Time:** 30 minutes | **Serves 2**

1 small red beet

1 cup cashews

½ cup olive oil

1 teaspoon salt

2 cups cooked quinoa

4 celery stalks, sliced into 4"-long sticks

4 medium carrots, peeled and sliced into 4"-long sticks

1 small cucumber, peeled and sliced into 4"-long sticks

1. Preheat oven to 400°F. Wrap beet in tinfoil and roast for 20–30 minutes or until fork-tender. Remove from heat and allow to cool.

2. In a large blender, combine beet, cashews, olive oil, and salt and blend on high until a creamy consistency develops, about 5 minutes.

3. Pour 1 cup quinoa into each of two serving bowls. Top each with equal amounts of hummus and place half the vegetable sticks over the top of each bowl. Serve cold.

PER SERVING   Calories: 1181 | Fat: 86.6 grams | Protein: 21.4 grams | Sodium: 1367 milligrams | Fiber: 13.6 grams | Carbohydrates: 81.5 grams | Sugar: 15.8 grams

POWER SOURCES

BEETS: betalain combats inflammatory compounds

OLIVE OIL: healthy fats improve cholesterol levels in the bloodstream

QUINOA: fiber supports healthy digestive system bacteria balance for improved immunity

CELERY: potassium supports healthy cardiovascular system functioning

Tex-Mex Taco Bowl

Prep Time: 5 minutes | **Cook Time:** 20 minutes | **Serves 2**

2 tablespoons olive oil, divided

2 whole-wheat tortillas, cut into 1"-thick strips

8 ounces extra-firm tofu, crumbled

1 cup corn

1 (8-ounce) can black beans, rinsed and drained

1 teaspoon salt

½ teaspoon cayenne

2 cups shredded lettuce

1 large tomato, chopped

½ cup nonfat yogurt

½ cup shredded Cheddar cheese

POWER SOURCES

TOFU: protein helps with muscle repair and plays a role in many processes in the body needed for proper metabolic function

TOMATO: lycopene combats free-radical damage and fights inflammation

BLACK BEANS: fiber supports healthy blood sugar levels

1 Coat a large skillet with 1 tablespoon olive oil and heat over medium heat. Add tortilla strips and cook until lightly browned and crisp, 3–5 minutes. Remove from skillet and place on paper towels to absorb excess moisture.

2 Add remaining 1 tablespoon olive oil to skillet and cook tofu crumbles until cooked through and lightly golden, about 7–10 minutes.

3 Add corn and black beans to skillet, season with salt and cayenne, and stir to heat through and thoroughly combine, about 5 minutes. Remove from heat.

4 Place equal amounts of tortilla strips in each of two serving bowls and top each with 1 cup lettuce. Spoon equal amounts of tofu mixture on top of lettuce, add half the tomatoes, and spoon ¼ cup yogurt on each bowl. Garnish each bowl with ¼ cup shredded Cheddar. Serve hot.

PER SERVING   Calories: 609 | Fat: 25.8 grams | Protein: 35.8 grams | Sodium: 1749 milligrams | Fiber: 14.5 grams | Carbohydrates: 59.9 grams | Sugar: 16.3 grams

Fruit-Quinoa Bowl with Pistachio Cream

Prep Time: 10 minutes | **Cook Time:** N/A | **Serves 2**

1 cup blueberries

1 cup sliced strawberries

1 cup peeled and chopped mango

1 teaspoon honey

½ cup organic apple juice

½ cup shelled pistachio nuts

1 tablespoon ground flaxseed

1 small avocado, peeled and pitted

2 cups cooked quinoa

2 kiwis, peeled and sliced

1 In a large bowl, combine the berries, mango, and honey and toss to combine thoroughly.

2 In a blender, combine apple juice, pistachios, and flaxseed and blend on high until all ingredients are broken down, about 2–4 minutes. Add avocado and blend on high until thoroughly combined and creamy, about 2 minutes.

3 Pour 1 cup quinoa into each of two serving bowls and top each with equal amounts of the berry mixture and avocado cream; garnish each bowl with half the kiwi slices. Serve cold.

PER SERVING   Calories: 731 | Fat: 28.2 grams | Protein: 19.3 grams | Sodium: 25 milligrams | Fiber: 21.0 grams | Carbohydrates: 105.7 grams | Sugar: 42.5 grams

POWER SOURCES

MANGO: vitamin C supports immune system functioning

KIWI: vitamin E prevents free-radical damage in DNA molecules for reduced inflammation

QUINOA: contains all essential amino acids for maximized muscle functioning and support

AVOCADO: monounsaturated fats support healthy blood lipid levels

Minestrone Soup Bowl

Prep Time: 10 minutes | **Cook Time:** 30 minutes | **Serves 4**

1 tablespoon olive oil

1 small yellow onion, peeled and chopped

2 medium carrots, peeled and chopped

1 clove garlic, chopped

2 teaspoons salt, divided

2 celery stalks, chopped

10 small tomatoes, chopped

½ cup chicken broth

1 teaspoon black pepper

1 (8-ounce) can kidney beans, rinsed and drained

2 cups cooked whole-wheat penne

3 cups spinach

¼ cup chopped fresh cilantro

1 In a large pot over medium-high heat, combine olive oil, onions, carrots, garlic, and 1 teaspoon salt and cook until vegetables are slightly softened, about 5–7 minutes. Remove from heat.

2 In a large blender, combine celery, tomatoes, broth, remaining 1 teaspoon salt, and pepper. Blend on high until all ingredients are broken down and thoroughly combined, about 2–3 minutes. Add contents of blender to pot.

3 Reduce heat to a simmer and add beans. Cook for 20 minutes, remove from heat, and stir in pasta and spinach until wilted.

4 Pour equal amounts of soup into each of two serving bowls. Garnish each bowl with ⅛ cup cilantro. Serve hot.

PER SERVING   Calories: 453 | Fat: 9.9 grams | Protein: 19.9 grams | Sodium: 2819 milligrams | Fiber: 20.0 grams | Carbohydrates: 82.2 grams | Sugar: 17.2 grams

POWER SOURCES

TOMATO: lycopene removes free radicals from the bloodstream

GARLIC: anti-inflammatory compounds fight inflammation

KIDNEY BEANS: vitamin B_6 contributes to white blood cell production

SPINACH: iron contributes to healthy oxygenation in blood

Marinated Tomatoes, Onions, and Cucumbers

Prep Time: 20 minutes | **Cook Time:** N/A | **Serves 2**

½ small red onion, peeled and sliced thin

1 small cucumber, peeled and sliced thin

2 small tomatoes, sliced thin

¼ cup apple cider vinegar

2 cups cooked quinoa

1 tablespoon olive oil

1 teaspoon salt

1 teaspoon pepper

1 small avocado, peeled, pitted, and sliced thin

1. In a large bowl, combine onion, cucumber, tomatoes, and vinegar. Refrigerate for 15 minutes.
2. Add quinoa to bowl, drizzle with olive oil, season with salt and pepper, and toss to combine.
3. Pour equal amounts of quinoa salad into each of two serving bowls. Top each bowl with half the avocado slices and serve cold.

PER SERVING   Calories: 434 | Fat: 19.4 grams | Protein: 11.0 grams | Sodium: 1187 milligrams | Fiber: 12.0 grams | Carbohydrates: 53.0 grams | Sugar: 6.1 grams

POWER SOURCES

TOMATO: vitamin C acts as a potent antioxidant for protection against free radicals

ONION: quercetin helps to safeguard cells against free-radical damage

AVOCADO: healthy fats reduce inflammation

Shrimp Stir-Fry

Prep Time: 5 minutes | **Cook Time:** 15 minutes | **Serves 2**

1 tablespoon sesame oil

1 cup peeled and chopped Vidalia onion

1 cup peeled and matchstick-sized-sliced carrots

1 cup pea pods

1 clove garlic, minced

1 cup mushrooms

½ cup sliced water chestnuts

1 pound shrimp, peeled and deveined

½ cup chicken broth

2 tablespoons low-sodium soy sauce

2 cups cooked wild rice

2 tablespoons sesame seeds

1 In a large skillet, combine sesame oil, onions, carrots, and pea pods and cook on medium heat until vegetables are softened, about 5 minutes.

2 Add garlic, mushrooms, water chestnuts, shrimp, and chicken broth to skillet. Cook until shrimp are cooked through, about 5–7 minutes.

3 Pour soy sauce into mixture and stir to combine thoroughly and heat through, about 2–3 minutes. Remove from heat.

4 Pour 1 cup rice into each of two serving bowls and top each with equal amounts of the stir-fry. Garnish each bowl with 1 tablespoon sesame seeds. Serve hot.

PER SERVING   Calories: 579 | Fat: 10.8 grams | Protein: 59.8 grams | Sodium: 1069 milligrams | Fiber: 9.5 grams | Carbohydrates: 63.6 grams | Sugar: 11.7 grams

POWER SOURCES

SESAME OIL: omega-3 fatty acids help reduce inflammation

PEA PODS: vitamin K helps with blood clotting

CARROT: beta carotene supports healthy regeneration of white blood cells

CHAPTER 12
Bowls for Better Digestion

Irritable bowel syndrome, colitis, diverticulitis, heartburn, constipation, cramping, bloating, and diarrhea are just a few of the most commonly experienced digestive conditions. Cleansing the digestive tract, improving the "good" bacteria that aid digestion, and restoring regularity can be done simply by improving the nutritional content in the food you consume every day. And by incorporating whole, clean foods such as fibrous fruits and vegetables, whole grains, and additions like nonfat yogurts that all contribute to the health of the digestive system, these problems can be resolved naturally.

Packed with probiotics, fiber, essential vitamins and minerals, and protective antioxidants, the healthy ingredients that are included in every power bowl recipe in this chapter make resolving common digestive issues simple and delicious. With digestive health restored, your entire body will benefit from improved immunity, reduced fatigue, maximized mental functioning, and a greater quality of life. So enjoy these breakfasts, lunches, dinners, and snacks that pack tons of digestion-focused nutrition into every last bite!

Ginger Chicken and Squash

Prep Time: 5 minutes | **Cook Time:** 20 minutes | **Serves 2**

1 tablespoon olive oil, divided

2 (4-ounce) chicken breasts

1 small acorn squash, peeled, seeded, and cut into ¼" cubes

1 small red bell pepper, seeded and cut into ¼" strips

1" gingerroot, peeled and minced

1 teaspoon salt

1 teaspoon pepper

2 cups couscous

2 cups spinach, chopped

½ cup crumbled feta cheese

1 Preheat oven to 375°F. Grease a 13" × 9" glass dish with ½ tablespoon olive oil and place chicken breasts in pan.

2 Scatter squash, peppers, and ginger around chicken. Then drizzle ½ tablespoon olive oil over chicken and vegetables and season with salt and pepper. Bake for 20 minutes or until chicken is cooked through and juices run clear.

3 In a large bowl, combine couscous, spinach, and feta and toss to combine.

4 Pour equal amounts of couscous into each of two serving bowls. Spoon equal amounts of the squash and peppers over couscous and top with 1 chicken breast for each bowl. Serve hot.

PER SERVING   Calories: 541 | Fat: 14.5 grams | Protein: 38.3 grams | Sodium: 1544 milligrams | Fiber: 6.7 grams | Carbohydrates: 64.0 grams | Sugar: 2.9 grams

POWER SOURCES

GINGER: anti-inflammatory compounds help alleviate inflammation in the digestive tract

CHICKEN: B vitamins support energy metabolism

SQUASH: vitamin A combats free-radical damage

BELL PEPPER: vitamin C increases immunity against infection

SPINACH: iron improves oxygenation in blood

✴ POWER BOWL PRIORITIES

Spicy foods, cruciferous vegetables, and even dairy products can cause digestive issues. Fortunately, it's easy to find replacements and alternatives that maintain the flavors of your favorite dishes without wreaking havoc on your digestive system. Swap cruciferous vegetables for leafy greens, dairy products for soy or almond-based alternatives, and use aromatic spices instead of spicy additions. By making these changes, you can still enjoy your power bowls with the added benefit of digestive relief.

Creamy Butternut Squash Soup

Prep Time: 10 minutes | **Cook Time:** 22 minutes | **Serves 2**

3 cups unsweetened vanilla almond milk

8 ounces crumbled silken tofu

2" gingerroot, peeled and chopped

1 tablespoon honey

3 teaspoons ground nutmeg, divided

2 small butternut squash, peeled, seeded, and cut into 1/2" cubes

1 cup plus 2 tablespoons nonfat yogurt, divided

2 cups cooked polenta

POWER SOURCES

YOGURT: probiotics promote healthy bacteria levels in the gut

GINGER: antibacterial compounds are thought to kill bacteria in the digestive system

POLENTA: adds natural carbohydrates for clean energy production

1 In a large pot over medium-high heat, combine almond milk, tofu, ginger, honey, and 1 teaspoon nutmeg and cook for 1–2 minutes.

2 Add squash to pot. Bring to a boil, reduce heat, and simmer for 20 minutes.

3 Remove pot from heat and set aside to cool for 5 minutes. Use an immersion blender on high to blend ingredients until broken down and thoroughly combined, about 2–3 minutes.

4 Add 1 cup yogurt and blend on high until all ingredients are well blended, about 1–2 minutes.

5 Pour 1 cup polenta into each of two serving bowls and top each with equal amounts of soup. Top each bowl with 1 tablespoon nonfat yogurt and sprinkle with 1 teaspoon nutmeg. Serve hot.

PER SERVING   Calories: 724 | Fat: 15.7 grams | Protein: 36.7 grams | Sodium: 372 milligrams | Fiber: 10.2 grams | Carbohydrates: 110.1 grams | Sugar: 24.9 grams

Spinach and Feta Meatballs with Rice Noodles

Prep Time: 10 minutes | **Cook Time:** 15 minutes | **Serves 2**

1 tablespoon olive oil

½ pound ground turkey

1 cup thawed and drained frozen spinach

1 large egg

¼ cup Greek yogurt

½ cup feta cheese

2 teaspoons salt, divided

2 teaspoons pepper, divided

2 teaspoons garlic powder, divided

2 teaspoons onion powder, divided

2 teaspoons dried oregano, divided

4 small tomatoes, chopped

2 cups cooked rice noodles

1 Preheat oven to 375°F. Coat a nonstick baking sheet with 1 tablespoon olive oil for meatballs. Set aside.

2 In a large bowl, combine turkey, spinach, egg, yogurt, and feta and stir to combine thoroughly. Add 1 teaspoon each of salt, pepper, garlic and onion powders, and oregano; stir to combine well.

3 Roll meat mixture into 20 (1") meatballs and place on prepared baking sheet. Cook for 15 minutes or until browned and cooked through. Remove from heat.

4 In a large bowl, combine tomatoes and remaining 1 teaspoon each of salt, pepper, garlic and onion powders, and oregano and toss to combine.

5 Pour 1 cup noodles into each of two serving bowls and top each with half the tomato sauce. Top each bowl with 10 meatballs. Serve hot.

PER SERVING   Calories: 610 | Fat: 25.1 grams | Protein: 34.6 grams | Sodium: 2877 milligrams | Fiber: 7.8 grams | Carbohydrates: 61.9 grams | Sugar: 8.3 grams

POWER SOURCES

SPINACH: fiber supports healthy digestive system functioning

RICE NOODLES: manganese acts to metabolize macronutrients

TOMATO: lycopene prevents cancerous cell changes in the colon

GREEK YOGURT: B vitamins contribute to enzymatic reactions related to the metabolism of fats

Tomato Soup with Kale and White Beans

Prep Time: 5 minutes | **Cook Time:** 25 minutes | **Serves 2**

- 8 small tomatoes, crushed
- 1 small yellow onion, peeled and chopped
- 1 garlic clove, chopped
- 1 cup chicken broth
- 2 cups chopped kale
- 1 teaspoon salt
- 1 teaspoon pepper
- 1 (16-ounce) can white beans, rinsed and drained
- 1 cup cooked quinoa
- 2 tablespoons chopped parsley

1 In a large pot over medium-high heat, combine tomatoes, onion, garlic, and chicken broth. Bring to a boil, then reduce heat to a simmer. Add kale to pot and cook for 15 minutes until all vegetables are tender.

2 Season with salt and pepper. Using an immersion blender on high, blend ingredients until broken down, about 2–3 minutes.

3 Add beans and quinoa to pot and stir to distribute throughout. Cook until heated through, about 5 minutes. Remove from heat.

4 Pour equal amounts of soup into each of two serving bowls. Garnish each bowl with 1 tablespoon chopped parsley. Serve hot or cold.

PER SERVING Calories: 432 | Fat: 2.8 grams | Protein: 23.7 grams | Sodium: 1666 milligrams | Fiber: 17.9 grams | Carbohydrates: 81.9 grams | Sugar: 13.2 grams

POWER SOURCES

TOMATO: lycopene acts as a potent antioxidant that protects the body from free-radical damage

GARLIC: antiviral compounds cleanse the gut of common viruses

KALE: fiber supports regularity

WHITE BEANS: B vitamins contribute to proper digestive-related metabolic processes

White Chicken Chili

Prep Time: 10 minutes | **Cook Time:** 15 minutes | **Serves 4**

1 tablespoon olive oil

1 clove garlic, minced

1 large red onion, peeled and chopped

1 (4-ounce) grilled chicken breast, chopped

1 (16-ounce) can great northern beans, rinsed and drained

4 small tomatoes, diced

1 teaspoon salt

1 tablespoon cumin

2 cups vegetable broth

2 cups spinach

1 cup nonfat Greek yogurt

1 In a large pot over medium-high heat, add olive oil, garlic, and onion and sauté until onion is translucent, about 5 minutes.

2 Add chicken, beans, and tomatoes and season with salt and cumin. Stir to combine. Add broth and bring soup to a boil. Reduce heat and simmer for 10 minutes or until all ingredients are fork-tender. Remove from heat.

3 Add spinach and stir until wilted. Cool for 5 minutes.

4 Pour equal amounts of soup into each of four serving bowls and garnish by spooning ¼ cup yogurt on top of each. Serve hot.

PER SERVING   Calories: 394 | Fat: 8.2 grams | Protein: 36.4 grams | Sodium: 2534 milligrams | Fiber: 13.3 grams | Carbohydrates: 49.2 grams | Sugar: 14.3 grams

POWER SOURCES

CHICKEN: B vitamins help convert food sources to energy

GREAT NORTHERN BEANS: fiber cleanses the digestive system and colon for reduced incidence of diverticulosis

YOGURT: potassium supports healthy muscle contraction in digestive system

TOMATO: vitamin C supports immune system functioning

✳ POWER BOWL PRIORITIES

While many processed and refined foods claim to provide the same nutritional benefits as their whole-food counterparts, the best bet is always natural. While the sugar, sodium, and nutrient content may seem to be comparable, the processing that is required for shelf-friendly foods minimizes the effectiveness of nutrients by destroying the molecular integrity of the nutrients or by adding synthetic additives that act as preservatives. By opting for foods that can be found in nature in their natural forms, your power bowl meals and your body will benefit!

Chicken Piccata with Zucchini Noodles

Prep Time: 5 minutes | **Cook Time:** 15 minutes | **Serves 2**

1 large zucchini

1 tablespoon olive oil

1 (4-ounce) chicken breast, halved lengthwise

½ cup lemon juice

1 tablespoon dried oregano

1 teaspoon salt

1 teaspoon garlic powder

POWER SOURCES

CHICKEN: protein supports healthy red blood cell production

LEMON: limonins safeguard tissues against damage by free radicals

ZUCCHINI: fiber helps aid in digestion

1 Spiralize zucchini into noodles in a large bowl. Set aside.

2 Coat a large skillet with olive oil and heat over medium heat. Add chicken breasts and cook for 5–7 minutes or until golden brown. Flip breasts, add lemon juice and oregano, and cook for 5–7 minutes or until chicken is cooked through and juices run clear. Season with salt and garlic powder.

3 Remove breasts from skillet and place on paper towels to drain.

4 Add zucchini noodles to skillet to heat through, about 1 minute. Remove from heat.

5 Pour equal amounts of zucchini noodles into each of two serving bowls and top each with 1 chicken breast half. Top each bowl with half the remaining pan juices. Serve hot.

PER SERVING   Calories: 150 | Fat: 6.0 grams | Protein: 14.4 grams | Sodium: 1175 milligrams | Fiber: 2.4 grams | Carbohydrates: 10.9 grams | Sugar: 5.3 grams

Berry Oatmeal with Ginger-Cardamom Cream

Prep Time: 5 minutes | **Cook Time:** N/A | **Serves 2**

1 cup blackberries

2 cups cooked oatmeal

1 cup blueberries

2 cups nonfat yogurt

2 teaspoons honey

2 teaspoons ground cardamom

2 teaspoons grated ginger

2 teaspoons cinnamon

1 cup sliced strawberries

POWER SOURCES

BERRIES: anthocyanins support immunity

OATS: fiber helps maintain steady blood sugar levels and helps with digestion

GINGER: gingerol minimizes nausea

YOGURT: probiotics support healthy levels of good bacteria in the gut

1 In a large bowl, mash blackberries. Add oatmeal and stir to combine. Add blueberries and fold in gently to distribute throughout oatmeal. Set aside.

2 In a small bowl, whisk together yogurt, honey, cardamom, ginger, and cinnamon until well blended.

3 Pour equal amounts of oatmeal into each of two serving bowls. Add equal amounts of cream on top, then garnish each bowl with ½ cup sliced strawberries. Serve cold.

PER SERVING   Calories: 410 | Fat: 2.0 grams | Protein: 21.3 grams | Sodium: 196 milligrams | Fiber: 14.3 grams | Carbohydrates: 83.3 grams | Sugar: 39.5 grams

Sweet and Spicy Creamy Chickpea Salad with Couscous

Prep Time: 5 minutes | **Cook Time:** N/A | **Serves 2**

1 cup yogurt

2 teaspoons honey

½ small red onion, peeled and minced

2 tablespoons ground flaxseed

1 cup cooked couscous

2 cups plus 2 tablespoons canned, drained, and rinsed chickpeas, divided

4 cups spinach

¼ cup raisins

1 In a large bowl, combine yogurt, honey, red onion, and flaxseed. Toss to coat all ingredients thoroughly.

2 Add couscous and 2 cups chickpeas and toss to combine thoroughly.

3 Place 2 cups spinach in each of two serving bowls, then add half the yogurt-coated couscous. Garnish each bowl with 1 tablespoon chickpeas and ⅛ cup raisins. Serve chilled.

PER SERVING   Calories: 518 | Fat: 9.5 grams | Protein: 22.5 grams | Sodium: 456 milligrams | Fiber: 15.6 grams | Carbohydrates: 87.0 grams | Sugar: 29.8 grams

POWER SOURCES

HONEY: natural antioxidants support cell health while removing free radicals from blood and tissue

CHICKPEAS: fiber aids in regularity for reduced incidence of constipation

SPINACH: iron improves oxygenation in blood

Spicy Chicken and Slaw Wraps with Edamame Rice

Prep Time: 10 minutes | **Cook Time:** N/A | **Serves 2**

1 cup nonfat plain yogurt

¼ teaspoon cayenne

1 teaspoon garlic powder

1 teaspoon grated ginger

1 teaspoon onion powder

1 teaspoon salt

1 (4-ounce) chicken breast, grilled and shredded

1 tablespoon sesame oil

½ cup shredded cabbage

½ cup peeled and shredded carrots

2 whole-wheat tortillas

2 cups rice

1 tablespoon low-sodium soy sauce

1 cup shelled and cooked edamame

1   In a large bowl, add yogurt, cayenne, garlic powder, ginger, onion powder, and salt and stir to combine. Add chicken and toss to coat. Add sesame oil, cabbage, and carrots and toss to coat.

2   Place tortillas on a flat surface and spoon half the chicken mixture into the center of each. Fold sides of tortillas in toward the center and tuck bottom of tortilla in as its rolled to enclose chicken mixture. Secure with toothpicks.

3   In a large bowl, combine rice, soy sauce, and edamame and toss to thoroughly combine.

4   Pour equal amounts of edamame rice into each of two serving bowls and top each bowl with 1 wrap. Serve warm or chilled.

PER SERVING   Calories: 650 | Fat: 18.3 grams | Protein: 34.5 grams | Sodium: 1711 milligrams | Fiber: 10.3 grams | Carbohydrates: 83.2 grams | Sugar: 10.5 grams

POWER SOURCES

YOGURT: probiotics support healthy levels of good bacteria in the gut

CABBAGE: sterols promote healthy cholesterol levels in the bloodstream

CARROT: beta carotene fights free-radical damage

Apple-Ginger Smoothie with Spinach and Green Tea

Prep Time: 5 minutes | **Cook Time:** N/A | **Serves 2**

3 cups cooled green tea

1" gingerroot, peeled and chopped

2 small Granny Smith apples, peeled, cored, and sliced

1 teaspoon honey

1 cup spinach

1 cup ice

2 sprigs fresh mint

POWER SOURCES

APPLE: fiber contributes to colon health by cleansing undigested debris

GINGER: anti-inflammatory compounds combat inflammation in tissues

SPINACH: iron promotes blood health

HONEY: natural antioxidants support cell health while removing free radicals from blood and tissue

1 In a large blender, combine green tea and ginger and blend on high until ginger is broken down, about 1 minute.

2 Add apples and honey and blend on high until broken down and combined, about 2 minutes.

3 Add spinach and blend on high until broken down and distributed throughout.

4 Add ice gradually while blending on high and blend until smooth.

5 Pour equal amounts of smoothie into each of two serving bowls. Top each bowl with 1 mint sprig. Serve cold.

PER SERVING   Calories: 94 | Fat: 0.2 grams | Protein: 0.9 grams | Sodium: 15 milligrams | Fiber: 3.9 grams | Carbohydrates: 24.9 grams | Sugar: 18.4 grams

Pomegranate-Pineapple Smoothie Bowl

Prep Time: 10 minutes | **Cook Time:** N/A | **Serves 2**

1 cup organic apple juice

1 cup plus 2 teaspoons pomegranate jewels, divided

1 cup plus 2 teaspoons chopped pineapple, divided

2 tablespoons ground flaxseed

½ cup spinach

2 cups plain kefir

1 cup ice

POWER SOURCES

POMEGRANATE: natural polyphenols protect liver and prostate cells from cancerous changes

KEFIR: probiotics improve healthy bacteria in the gut for improved digestion

APPLE JUICE: vitamin C supports a healthy immune system needed to combat infection

1   In a large blender, combine apple juice, 1 cup pomegranate jewels, 1 cup pineapple, and flaxseed and blend on high until all ingredients are broken down and well blended, about 2–3 minutes.

2   Add spinach and blend on high until all leaves are broken down and thoroughly combined, about 2–3 minutes.

3   Add kefir and blend on high until thoroughly combined, about 1 minute.

4   Add ice gradually while blending on high and blend until smooth.

5   Pour equal amounts of smoothie into each of two serving bowls. Top each bowl with 1 teaspoon pomegranate jewels and 1 teaspoon chopped pineapple. Serve chilled.

PER SERVING   Calories: 387 | Fat: 11.2 grams | Protein: 11.8 grams | Sodium: 140 milligrams | Fiber: 10.7 grams | Carbohydrates: 62.5 grams | Sugar: 47.1 grams

Cream of Asparagus Soup with Quinoa

Prep Time: 10 minutes | **Cook Time:** 10 minutes | **Serves 2**

1 tablespoon olive oil

1 clove garlic, minced

1 pound asparagus, trimmed

½ cup vegetable broth

2 cups kefir

1 teaspoon salt

1 cup cooked quinoa

POWER SOURCES

GARLIC: allicin combats dangerous triglycerides and cholesterol levels

KEFIR: probiotics support the immune system's defenses in the gut

QUINOA: fiber supports regularity

1   Coat a large skillet with olive oil and heat over medium heat. Add garlic and asparagus and sauté for 3 minutes or until asparagus begins to wilt.

2   Add vegetable broth to skillet and steam asparagus for 5 minutes or until asparagus is fork-tender. Remove from heat and allow to cool for 5 minutes.

3   Pour asparagus, garlic, and broth into a blender and blend on high until asparagus is broken down, about 2–3 minutes.

4   Add kefir to blender, season with salt, and blend on high until thoroughly combined.

5   Pour ½ cup quinoa into each of two serving bowls and top each with half the soup. Serve warm or chilled.

PER SERVING   Calories: 367 | Fat: 14.8 grams | Protein: 17.2 grams | Sodium: 1532 milligrams | Fiber: 10.4 grams | Carbohydrates: 44.8 grams | Sugar: 17.6 grams

CHAPTER 13
Bowls for Healthy Skin

Around the world, trillions of dollars are spent on pills, potions, and creams that promise to give you beautiful skin, but those promises often fall flat and leave consumers disappointed. Even worse, some products contain harsh and sometimes harmful chemicals, additives, and synthetic ingredients that can wreak havoc on your overall health. Fortunately, the power bowls found in this chapter can restore and rejuvenate your skin.

With whole foods that hydrate, provide protection against oxidative and free-radical damage, and ensure that your body's needs for essential nutrients are met, these power bowls are simple, nutritious, and delicious. Beauty begins on the inside, and in these bowls, B vitamins; vitamins A, C, D, E, and K; and minerals like calcium, iron, and silica combine with potent antioxidants such as resveratrol to promote the healthy regeneration of skin cells while repairing and rejuvenating the existing ones. So eat for health and enjoy the benefits of beauty with every one of these delicious and nutritious power bowls.

Cucumber-Grape Salad with Feta

Prep Time: 10 minutes | **Cook Time:** N/A | **Serves 2**

2 small English cucumbers, ends removed and chopped

1 small tomato, chopped

1 small red onion, peeled and minced

1 cup halved seedless red grapes

2 tablespoons organic apple cider vinegar

2 tablespoons aloe vera juice

2 cups chopped spinach

2 tablespoons olive oil

½ cup feta cheese

1 cup cooked quinoa

1. In a large bowl, combine cucumber, tomato, onion, grapes, vinegar, and aloe vera. Toss to combine.
2. Add spinach, olive oil, and feta and toss to combine.
3. Place ½ cup quinoa in each of two serving bowls and layer equal amounts of salad over top. Serve chilled.

PER SERVING   Calories: 463 | Fat: 22.8 grams | Protein: 13.6 grams | Sodium: 384 milligrams | Fiber: 6.5 grams | Carbohydrates: 53.7 grams | Sugar: 23.3 grams

❋ POWER BOWL PRIORITIES

While it may be tempting to indulge in sweet treats like baked goods, sweetened smoothies, and sugary dairy dishes, the processed sugars used in these foods can be detrimental to the appearance of your skin. By opting for naturally sweetened treats like smoothies, fruit salads, and fruit-based desserts, you can satisfy your sweet tooth while satisfying the needs of your skin cells' needs.

POWER SOURCES

ALOE VERA JUICE: vitamin E supports healthy skin cell regeneration

ONION: allicin acts as an antioxidant for protection against oxidative damage in cells

GRAPES: resveratrol acts as a potent antioxidant against free-radical damage

Powerful Peach Parfait

Prep Time: 5 minutes | **Cook Time:** N/A | **Serves 2**

2 cups nonfat yogurt

1 tablespoon honey

1 cup rolled oats

2 cups halved seedless green grapes

2 small peaches, pitted and sliced

1 cup sliced strawberries

1 teaspoon cinnamon

1. In a large bowl, combine yogurt and honey and stir to combine.
2. Fold oats into yogurt and stir to coat. Add grapes and peaches to yogurt-oat mixture and toss to combine.
3. Pour equal amounts of yogurt, oats, and fruit into each of two serving bowls and top each bowl with ½ cup strawberry slices. Sprinkle each bowl with ½ teaspoon cinnamon and serve cold.

PER SERVING   Calories: 506 | Fat: 3.1 grams | Protein: 22.3 grams | Sodium: 194 milligrams | Fiber: 9.8 grams | Carbohydrates: 101.9 grams | Sugar: 66.1 grams

POWER SOURCES

PEACH: vitamin A combats free-radical damage in skin cells

GRAPES: resveratrol acts as a potent antioxidant against free-radical damage

OATS: fiber promotes healthy blood pressure levels

YOGURT: calcium regulates sleep and wake cycles, which help repair and retain healthy skin

Fiery Sweet Potato Bisque

Prep Time: 5 minutes | **Cook Time:** 15 minutes | **Serves 2**

4 cups water

2 large sweet potatoes, peeled and chopped

2 cups spinach

1 teaspoon ground nutmeg

2 teaspoons cayenne

4 cups vanilla kefir

2 tablespoons aloe vera juice

½ teaspoon cinnamon, divided

POWER SOURCES

KEFIR: probiotics contribute to healthy immune system functioning in the gut

SPINACH: fiber supports healthy blood pressure levels

ALOE VERA JUICE: polyphenolic compounds help to protect skin cells against oxidative stress

1 In a large pot over high heat, combine water and sweet potatoes. Cook until sweet potatoes are fork-tender, about 10 minutes.

2 Add spinach and stir until wilted. Remove pot from heat, drain, then return sweet potatoes and spinach to pot.

3 Sprinkle potatoes and spinach with nutmeg and cayenne and add kefir.

4 Add aloe vera to pot. Using an immersion blender, blend ingredients on high until fully broken down and thoroughly combined, about 2–3 minutes.

5 Pour equal amounts of bisque into each of two serving bowls. Garnish each bowl with ¼ teaspoon cinnamon. Serve hot or cold.

PER SERVING   Calories: 436 | Fat: 8.7 grams | Protein: 18.9 grams | Sodium: 251 milligrams | Fiber: 8.9 grams | Carbohydrates: 78.1 grams | Sugar: 52.3 grams

✷ POWER BOWL PRIORITIES

Everyone loves feeling the warmth of the sun, but with the growing awareness of the harm that can be caused by unprotected sun exposure, sunlight, the primary source of vitamin D, is being increasingly avoided. As a result, this crucial vitamin must be obtained through nutrition. With a major role in teeth and bone formation, regularity of heartbeat, and even hormone production within the thyroid gland, vitamin D must be consumed through lean meats, vegetables, and fortified dairy and grains . . . all of which are found in the power bowls throughout the book.

Chimichurri Shrimp with Rice Noodles

Prep Time: 5 minutes | **Cook Time:** 15 minutes | **Serves 2**

- 1 tablespoon olive oil
- 1 clove garlic, minced
- 1 small yellow onion, peeled and diced
- ½ small red bell pepper, seeded and chopped
- ½ small green bell pepper, seeded and chopped
- 1 pound shrimp, peeled and deveined
- 1 tablespoon salt-free Cajun seasoning
- ¼ teaspoon cayenne
- 1 teaspoon salt
- 1 small tomato, diced
- 2 cups cooked rice noodles

1. In a large skillet over medium heat, add olive oil, garlic, onion, and peppers. Cook until vegetables are softened, about 5–7 minutes.
2. Add shrimp to skillet and sprinkle with Cajun seasoning, cayenne, and salt. Cook until shrimp are cooked through, about 5–7 minutes.
3. Add tomatoes to skillet and toss to combine. Remove from heat.
4. Place 1 cup rice noodles in each of two serving bowls and top each with equal amounts of shrimp mixture. Serve hot.

PER SERVING   Calories: 455 | Fat: 5.9 grams | Protein: 49.8 grams | Sodium: 1468 milligrams | Fiber: 3.4 grams | Carbohydrates: 48.9 grams | Sugar: 3.4 grams

POWER SOURCES

BELL PEPPER: vitamin C combats free-radical damage

ONION: quercetin helps to safeguard cells against free-radical damage

TOMATO: vitamin A protects skin cells from UV radiation damage

California Quinoa Salad

Prep Time: 10 minutes | **Cook Time:** N/A | **Serves 2**

1 tablespoon olive oil

2 tablespoons aloe vera juice

2 tablespoons balsamic vinegar

1 teaspoon salt

1 small English cucumber, chopped

1 small tomato, chopped

1 cup halved seedless red grapes

8 ounces extra-firm tofu, cut into ¼" cubes

2 cups chopped romaine lettuce

2 cups cooked quinoa

1 small avocado, peeled, pitted and sliced

1 In a large bowl, combine olive oil, aloe vera, vinegar, and salt and whisk to combine.

2 Add cucumber, tomatoes, grapes, and tofu and toss to coat.

3 Add 1 cup romaine on left side of each serving bowl, then add 1 cup quinoa on right side of each bowl. Layer equal amounts of tofu mixture over top of each bowl. Garnish each with half the avocado slices. Serve chilled.

PER SERVING   Calories: 596 | Fat: 25.7 grams | Protein: 23.2 grams | Sodium: 1199 milligrams | Fiber: 13.3 grams | Carbohydrates: 72.0 grams | Sugar: 19.9 grams

POWER SOURCES

AVOCADO: healthy fats support oil balance in skin's surface

GRAPES: resveratrol acts as a potent antioxidant against free-radical damage

TOFU: proteins contribute to the proper metabolism of energy for cells

Apple-Pear-Pecan Salad

Prep Time: 5 minutes | **Cook Time:** N/A | **Serves 2**

4 cups mixed greens

1 small apple, cored and chopped

1 small pear, cored and chopped

½ cup cranberries

2 tablespoons olive oil

2 tablespoons balsamic vinegar

1 tablespoon honey

2 tablespoons ground flaxseed

1 cup crushed pecans

½ cup crumbled feta cheese

1 In a large bowl, combine greens, apple, pear, and cranberries and toss to combine.

2 In a small bowl, whisk together olive oil, vinegar, honey, and flaxseed until thoroughly combined. Add to greens and toss to coat.

3 Pour equal amounts of salad into each of two serving bowls and garnish each bowl with ½ cup crushed pecans and ¼ cup feta. Serve chilled.

PER SERVING   Calories: 783 | Fat: 60.9 grams | Protein: 13.4 grams | Sodium: 415 milligrams | Fiber: 13.8 grams | Carbohydrates: 52.0 grams | Sugar: 32.0 grams

POWER SOURCES

APPLE: quercetin combats free-radical damage

CRANBERRIES: anthocyanins prevent inflammation and redness in skin's surface

GREENS: iron promotes blood flow and oxygen delivery throughout the bloodstream

Spicy Gazpacho

Prep Time: 2 hours | **Cook Time:** 10 minutes | **Serves 4**

1 tablespoon olive oil

1 garlic clove, minced

1 cup peeled and chopped Vidalia onion

1 small green bell pepper, seeded and chopped

6 small tomatoes (2 crushed, 4 chopped), divided

1 teaspoon salt

¼ teaspoon cayenne

2 cups spinach

4 cups vegetable broth

1 small English cucumber, chopped

1 In a large pot over medium-high heat, combine olive oil, garlic, onions, peppers, and crushed tomatoes. Season with salt and cayenne and cook until vegetables are softened, about 5–7 minutes. Add spinach and stir until leaves are wilted, about 1–2 minutes. Remove from heat.

2 Add vegetable broth and chopped tomatoes and stir to combine.

3 Pour equal amounts of soup into each of four serving bowls. Top each with chopped cucumbers. Refrigerate for 1–2 hours. Serve chilled.

PER SERVING   Calories: 200 | Fat: 7.2 grams | Protein: 5.5 grams | Sodium: 3085 milligrams | Fiber: 6.6 grams | Carbohydrates: 32.4 grams | Sugar: 17.8 grams

POWER SOURCES

TOMATO: vitamin C combats free-radical damage in skin cells

GARLIC: anti-inflammatory benefits reduce inflammation in cells and tissues

BELL PEPPER: antioxidants safeguard cell health

Cucumber-Margherita Salad

Prep Time: 5 minutes | **Cook Time:** N/A | **Serves 2**

4 cups spinach

1 cup cooked quinoa

1 small English cucumber, chopped

2 tablespoons olive oil

2 large tomatoes, sliced

4 ounces mozzarella, sliced

¼ cup chopped fresh basil

1 teaspoon salt

2 tablespoons balsamic vinegar

1 In a large bowl, combine spinach, quinoa, cucumbers, and olive oil and toss to combine and coat evenly.

2 Pour equal amounts of salad into each of two serving bowls and top each with equal amounts of tomato slices. Top each with 2 ounces mozzarella slices, ⅛ cup basil, and ½ teaspoon salt; drizzle each with 1 tablespoon balsamic vinegar. Serve chilled.

PER SERVING   Calories: 483 | Fat: 25.2 grams | Protein: 22.5 grams | Sodium: 1617 milligrams | Fiber: 6.9 grams | Carbohydrates: 40.8 grams | Sugar: 12.0 grams

POWER SOURCES

SPINACH: vitamin K supports the immune system

TOMATO: vitamin C combats free-radical damage in skin cells

MOZZARELLA: protein provides strength for skin cell membranes for skin tightness

BASIL: vitamin A combats pollutant damage to skin cells

CUCUMBER: potassium maintains fluid balance in cells and tissues

Grape-Mandarin Chicken Salad

Prep Time: 5 minutes | **Cook Time:** N/A | **Serves 2**

2 tablespoons sesame oil

1 tablespoon ground flaxseed

2 tablespoons honey, divided

4 cups mixed greens

1 cup nonfat yogurt

1 (4-ounce) chicken breast, grilled and shredded

1 stalk celery, chopped

1 cup halved seedless red grapes

2 mandarin oranges, peeled, seeded, and sectioned

1 In a large bowl, combine oil, flaxseed, and 1 tablespoon honey and whisk together. Add greens and toss to coat.

2 In a large bowl, combine yogurt and 1 tablespoon honey and whisk to combine.

3 Pour equal amounts of greens into each of two serving bowls and top each with half the chicken, celery, and fruit; garnish each with half the honey yogurt. Serve chilled.

PER SERVING Calories: 426 | Fat: 15.6 grams | Protein: 22.1 grams | Sodium: 179 milligrams | Fiber: 4.3 grams | Carbohydrates: 54.8 grams | Sugar: 46.5 grams

POWER SOURCES

GRAPES: anthocyanins regulate blood sugar levels

ORANGE: vitamin C strengthens skin cell membranes and minimizes wrinkles

CHICKEN: protein supports the metabolic processes that convert foods to usable energy

GREENS: iron supports healthy blood oxygenation levels

YOGURT: B vitamins support healthy cell regeneration

Pumpkin Pie Smoothie Bowl

Prep Time: 2 minutes | **Cook Time:** N/A | **Serves 2**

3 cups vanilla kefir

2 tablespoons ground flaxseed

1 teaspoon cinnamon

1 teaspoon cloves

1 teaspoon maple syrup

1 tablespoon aloe vera juice

1 (10-ounce) can organic pumpkin purée

1 cup ice

2 tablespoons roasted pumpkin seeds

1 In a large blender, combine kefir and flaxseed and blend on high until thoroughly combined, about 2–3 minutes.

2 Add cinnamon, cloves, and maple syrup and blend on high until combined, about 1 minute.

3 Add aloe vera and pumpkin purée and blend on high until thoroughly combined, about 2–3 minutes.

4 Add ice gradually while blending on high and blend until smooth.

5 Pour equal amounts of smoothie into each of two serving bowls. Garnish each bowl with 1 tablespoon pumpkin seeds. Serve cold.

PER SERVING   Calories: 383 | Fat: 12.7 grams | Protein: 18.0 grams | Sodium: 138 milligrams | Fiber: 12.3 grams | Carbohydrates: 57.5 grams | Sugar: 42.2 grams

POWER SOURCES

PUMPKIN: vitamin A combats free-radical damage to maintain health of skin cells

CINNAMON: anti-inflammatory benefits minimize inflammation and irritation

KEFIR: probiotics promote the growth of healthy bacteria in the gut for optimal nutrient absorption

Grape-Pear Cream Smoothie Bowl

Prep Time: 5 minutes | **Cook Time:** N/A | **Serves 2**

2 cups cooled green tea

1 tablespoon grated ginger

1 tablespoon aloe vera juice

1 tablespoon ground flaxseed

1 cup spinach

2 cups seedless Concord grapes

2 small pears, cored and chopped

2 cups vanilla kefir

1 cup ice

2 sprigs fresh mint

1 In a large blender, combine green tea, ginger, aloe vera, flaxseed, and spinach and blend on high until spinach and ginger are fully broken down, about 1–2 minutes.

2 Add grapes and pears and blend on high until all ingredients are broken down and thoroughly combined, about 2 minutes.

3 Add kefir and blend on high until well blended, about 1 minute.

4 Add ice gradually while blending on high and blend until smooth.

5 Pour equal amounts of smoothie into each of two serving bowls and garnish each bowl with 1 mint sprig.

PER SERVING   Calories: 389 | Fat: 5.6 grams | Protein: 10.8 grams | Sodium: 104 milligrams | Fiber: 9.4 grams | Carbohydrates: 79.7 grams | Sugar: 62.1 grams

POWER SOURCES

GRAPES: resveratrol acts as a potent antioxidant against free-radical damage

GINGER: anti-inflammatory compounds reduce inflammation and redness

SPINACH: fiber promotes healthy blood pressure

CHAPTER 14
Bowls for Antiaging

As we age, the body and mind can be strengthened or challenged, and the quality of the nutrients you consume can have a major impact on your body's ability to restore and replenish the cells responsible for everything from muscle strength to memory. This is why a diet of whole natural foods that provide essential vitamins and minerals is a must.

By including nutrient-dense foods like fresh fruits and vegetables, lean protein, whole grains, and healthy additions, each of the power bowls in this chapter is designed to give you antiaging benefits that ensure your nutrient needs are met. Here you'll find recipes packed full of B vitamins for brain health, iron for optimized oxygen delivery, and calcium for better bone health . . . and these are just a few of the nutrients that can easily be deficient when an inadequate diet is consumed daily.

Arguably, the most beneficial aspect of the nutritious recipes in this chapter are the antioxidant benefits that are provided by their ingredients. These antioxidants help to safeguard the cells of the brain, heart, nervous system, muscles, bones, and digestive system against degradation and damage, which helps improve immunity and strengthen the systems that contribute to overall health. You'll almost feel yourself getting younger with every bowl!

Cucumber-Melon Smoothie Bowl

Prep Time: 5 minutes | **Cook Time:** N/A | **Serves 2**

1 cup cooled green tea

1" gingerroot, peeled and chopped

1 teaspoon honey

1 small English cucumber, chopped

1 cup chopped honeydew melon

1 cup chopped cantaloupe

1 cup plus 2 tablespoons nonfat
   Greek yogurt, divided

1 cup ice

POWER SOURCES

CUCUMBER: potassium helps your body maintain adequate hydration in cells and tissues

CANTALOUPE: vitamin C boosts immune system functioning and vitamin A protects eye cells from oxidative damage

GINGER: anti-inflammatory compounds combat inflammation

1 In a large blender, combine green tea, ginger, and honey and blend on high until ginger is broken down and incorporated, about 1–2 minutes.

2 Add cucumber, melon, and cantaloupe and blend on high until all ingredients are thoroughly combined, about 2 minutes.

3 Add 1 cup yogurt and blend on high until thoroughly combined, about 1 minute.

4 Add ice gradually while blending on high and blend until smooth.

5 Pour equal amounts of smoothie into each of two serving bowls and top each bowl with 1 tablespoon yogurt. Serve chilled.

PER SERVING Calories: 166 | Fat: 0.3 grams | Protein: 15.4 grams | Sodium: 86 milligrams | Fiber: 2.2 grams | Carbohydrates: 28.2 grams | Sugar: 23.7 grams

✹ POWER BOWL PRIORITIES

Illnesses, diseases, and conditions related to the eyes can strike anyone of any age. Whether you're dealing with congenital cataracts that develop in the womb or macular degeneration that can occur in older ages, the importance of nutrition for eye health is extraordinary. With vitamin A providing antioxidants that protect against free-radical damage, B vitamins that reduce eye fatigue and ward off cataract formation, and vitamin C for overall improvement of immune system functioning for reduced illness and disease, natural foods such as lean meats, sweet potatoes and leafy greens, and citrus fruits can all help the eyes naturally!

"Chocolate" Chia Pudding

Prep Time: 5 minutes | **Cook Time:** N/A | **Serves 2**

6 dates, pitted

1 tablespoon honey

4 cups vanilla kefir

½ cup plus 2 teaspoons chia seeds, divided

2 tablespoons plus 2 teaspoons ground flaxseed, divided

1 cup ice

POWER SOURCES

CHIA SEEDS: fiber provides improved regularity

HONEY: natural antioxidants support cell health while removing free radicals from blood and tissue

FLAXSEED: omega-3s support brain and muscle health

1 In a large blender, combine dates, honey, and kefir and blend on high until dates are broken down, about 2–3 minutes.

2 Add ½ cup chia seeds and 2 tablespoons flaxseed and blend on high until thoroughly combined, about 1–2 minutes.

3 Add ice gradually while blending on high and blend until smooth.

4 Pour equal amounts of smoothie into each of two serving bowls. Garnish each bowl with 1 teaspoon chia seeds and 1 teaspoon flaxseed. Serve chilled.

PER SERVING   Calories: 843 | Fat: 27.2 grams | Protein: 27.6 grams | Sodium: 180 milligrams | Fiber: 27.2 grams | Carbohydrates: 138.2 grams | Sugar: 102.5 grams

☀ POWER BOWL PRIORITIES

The same little seeds that made the windowsill-adorning Chia Pets a nationally recognized name can contribute astounding amounts of natural nutrition to every one of your favorite power bowls. With omegas and natural antioxidants that protect and promote health and healing, these tiny seeds also keep you full for hours. Because the seeds turn into a fibrous gel in the digestive system, they trigger the brain to report a feeling of fullness while providing the body and mind with sustained energy throughout the day.

Sweet and Spicy Mahi-Mahi Salad

Prep Time: 5 minutes | **Cook Time:** 10 minutes | **Serves 2**

1 tablespoon olive oil

2 small jalapeños, seeded and minced

2 (4-ounce) mahi-mahi fillets

1 teaspoon salt

1 cup nonfat yogurt

2 tablespoons honey

1 small cucumber, peeled and chopped

2 small tomatoes, chopped

½ small red onion, peeled and sliced

4 cups romaine lettuce

1 Coat a large skillet with olive oil and heat over medium heat. Add jalapeño and mahi-mahi fillets and cook for 4–5 minutes. Flip fillets and use a spatula to crush and shred mahi-mahi. Season fish with salt, then stir mahi-mahi and jalapeño mixture. Cook for 4–5 minutes until mahi-mahi is cooked through and well combined with jalapeños. Remove from heat.

2 In a large bowl, whisk together yogurt and honey. Add cucumbers, tomatoes, and red onion and toss to coat.

3 Add 2 cups romaine to each of two serving bowls and top each with equal amounts of vegetable mixture. Top each bowl with half the fish and jalapeño mixture. Serve chilled.

PER SERVING   Calories: 318 | Fat: 6.2 grams | Protein: 29.6 grams | Sodium: 1364 milligrams | Fiber: 4.3 grams | Carbohydrates: 37.1 grams | Sugar: 32.3 grams

POWER SOURCES

MAHI-MAHI: protein supports the metabolism of food to usable energy

CUCUMBER: potassium maintains fluid balance in cells and tissues

TOMATO: vitamin A protects skin cells from UV damage

Asian Salmon with Red Pepper Quinoa

Prep Time: 10 minutes | **Cook Time:** 15 minutes | **Serves 2**

2 cups spinach

2 (6-ounce) salmon fillets

1 tablespoon honey

1 tablespoon low-sodium soy sauce

2 cups cooked quinoa

1 tablespoon sesame oil

1 small red bell pepper, seeded and chopped

2 tablespoons chopped scallions

1 Preheat oven to 400°F. Line a 13" × 9" pan with aluminum foil. Scatter spinach leaves on foil and place salmon fillets on top of spinach.

2 Drizzle honey and soy sauce on salmon. Bake for 15 minutes or until salmon is cooked through and flaky. Remove from heat and set aside.

3 In a large bowl, combine quinoa, sesame oil, and chopped peppers. Toss to combine thoroughly.

4 Pour equal amounts of red pepper–quinoa mixture into each of two serving bowls and top each with 1 salmon fillet and half the spinach. Garnish each bowl with 1 tablespoon chopped scallions. Serve warm.

POWER SOURCES

SALMON: omega-3s provide healthy fats for optimal brain functioning

BELL PEPPER: vitamin C promotes healthy cell regeneration

QUINOA: fiber promotes steady bloody pressure

PER SERVING   Calories: 548 | Fat: 15.0 grams | Protein: 44.9 grams | Sodium: 419 milligrams | Fiber: 6.6 grams | Carbohydrates: 51.3 grams | Sugar: 11.4 grams

Spicy Spinach, Sausage, and Mushroom Sauté

Prep Time: 5 minutes | **Cook Time:** 15 minutes | **Serves 4**

1 tablespoon olive oil

½ pound chopped turkey sausage

1 cup chopped mushrooms

1 garlic clove, minced

2 cups spinach

2 cups cooked quinoa

4 cups egg whites

¼ teaspoon cayenne

4 tablespoons crumbled feta cheese, divided

1 Coat a large skillet with olive oil and heat over medium heat. Add sausage and mushrooms and cook until sausage is cooked through, about 5–7 minutes.

2 Add garlic, spinach, and quinoa to skillet and toss to heat through until spinach is wilted, about 2 minutes.

3 Pour egg whites and cayenne over sausage and vegetable mixture and stir as whites cook and harden, about 5 minutes. Remove from heat.

4 Pour equal amounts of egg mixture into each of four serving bowls. Sprinkle 1 tablespoon feta over top of each bowl and serve hot.

PER SERVING   Calories: 851 | Fat: 27.7 grams | Protein: 83.3 grams | Sodium: 1740 milligrams | Fiber: 6.3 grams | Carbohydrates: 48.3 grams | Sugar: 6.7 grams

POWER SOURCES

SPINACH: vitamin K supports the immune system

EGG WHITES: choline supports brain health

GARLIC: allicin combats dangerous triglycerides and cholesterol levels

Tandoori Chicken Salad with Couscous

Prep Time: 5 minutes | **Cook Time:** N/A | **Serves 2**

2 cups nonfat Greek yogurt

1 tablespoon honey

1 tablespoon grated ginger

1 tablespoon ground turmeric

2 teaspoons garlic powder

2 teaspoons salt

¼ teaspoon cayenne

2 stalks celery, chopped

1 cup halved red seedless grapes

½ cup cooked couscous

1 (4-ounce) chicken breast, grilled and shredded

2 large whole-wheat pitas

¼ cup golden raisins

1. In a large bowl, combine yogurt, honey, ginger, turmeric, garlic powder, salt, and cayenne and whisk to combine.

2. Add celery, grapes, couscous, and chicken and toss to coat and combine thoroughly.

3. Open pita halves and roughly tear the pita halves into 1" squares, then place the torn pitas into each of two serving bowls. Spoon even amounts of chicken salad mixture into each bowl. Garnish each bowl with ⅛ cup raisins. Serve chilled.

PER SERVING Calories: 575 | Fat: 2.3 grams | Protein: 45.3 grams | Sodium: 2743 milligrams | Fiber: 8.8 grams | Carbohydrates: 97.2 grams | Sugar: 41.3 grams

POWER SOURCES

CHICKEN: protein supports healthy red blood cell regeneration

TURMERIC: anti-inflammatory benefits minimize inflammation within cells and tissues

YOGURT: calcium supports health of bones and teeth

Grape-Berry Tofu Smoothie

Prep Time: 5 minutes | **Cook Time:** N/A | **Serves 2**

1 cup organic apple juice

1½ tablespoons grated ginger, divided

1 cup seedless green grapes

1 cup strawberries, tops removed

1 cup blackberries

8 ounces silken tofu

1 teaspoon honey

1 cup ice

POWER SOURCES

GRAPES: antioxidants support cognitive functioning

STRAWBERRIES: anthocyanins provide antioxidant protection against free-radical damage

TOFU: protein supports healthy muscle contractions

1 In a large blender, combine apple juice and 1 tablespoon ginger and blend on high until well combined, about 1 minute.

2 Add grapes and berries and blend on high until fruit is broken down and thoroughly combined, about 2 minutes.

3 Add tofu and honey to blender and blend on high until all ingredients are thoroughly combined, about 1–2 minutes.

4 Add ice gradually while blending on high and blend until smooth.

5 Pour equal amounts of smoothie into each of two serving bowls. Garnish each bowl with ¼ tablespoon ginger. Serve chilled.

PER SERVING Calories: 340 | Fat: 9.7 grams | Protein: 20.1 grams | Sodium: 23 milligrams | Fiber: 8.9 grams | Carbohydrates: 48.6 grams | Sugar: 33.6 grams

✳ POWER BOWL PRIORITIES

Not only can delicious blueberries, blackberries, strawberries, and raspberries add tons of flavor to your smoothies, snacks, and salads, but they can also improve your breathing. These power bowl ingredients contain potent anthocyanins that color each beautiful berry with its unique hue and antioxidants that specifically target the respiratory system. Safeguarding every component of the lungs and airways against debris, toxins, and harmful free radicals, these tasty treats make every berry-filled power bowl a delicious way to breathe better every day.

Mixed-Green Salad with Balsamic-Berry Dressing

Prep Time: 5 minutes | **Cook Time:** N/A | **Serves 2**

1 cup raspberries

1 cup blackberries

2 tablespoons ground flaxseed

2 tablespoons balsamic vinegar

4 cups mixed greens

1 small red onion, peeled and minced

1 small English cucumber, chopped

1 cup shelled and chopped walnuts

1   In a large blender, combine berries, flaxseed, and vinegar and blend on high until berries are broken down, about 2 minutes.

2   In a large bowl, combine mixed greens, onions, and cucumber and toss to combine.

3   Pour contents of blender into salad and toss to coat.

4   Pour equal amounts of salad into each of two serving bowls and garnish each bowl with ½ cup crushed walnuts. Serve chilled.

PER SERVING   Calories: 452 | Fat: 34.3 grams | Protein: 12.3 grams | Sodium: 75 milligrams | Fiber: 12.6 grams | Carbohydrates: 31.7 grams | Sugar: 13.3 grams

POWER SOURCES

GREENS: fiber promotes healthy insulin levels in the bloodstream to regulate blood sugar levels

CUCUMBER: potassium supports proper nervous system functioning

BERRIES: antioxidants protect against free-radical damage

WALNUTS: omega-3s and -6s support proper brain functioning and protect against brain cell degeneration

VINEGAR: enzymes provide protection against microbes, viruses, and bacterial infections

Spinach and Feta Chicken with Creamy Wild Rice

Prep Time: 10 minutes | **Cook Time:** 20 minutes | **Serves 2**

2 (4-ounce) chicken breasts, butterflied

2 cups chopped spinach

½ cup crumbled feta

2 teaspoons salt, divided

1 teaspoon garlic powder

2 cups cooked wild rice

2 small tomatoes, chopped

1 cup nonfat Greek yogurt

1 cup nonfat yogurt

1 teaspoon pepper

1. Preheat oven to 375°F.
2. Place butterflied chicken breasts open-faced in a 9" × 9" pan. Layer chicken with spinach and feta. Sprinkle top of chicken with 1 teaspoon salt and garlic powder and bake for 15–20 minutes or until chicken is cooked through and juices run clear.
3. In a large bowl, combine wild rice, tomatoes, yogurts, remaining 1 teaspoon salt, and pepper and toss to combine and coat thoroughly.
4. Pour equal amounts of rice mixture into each of two serving bowls. Top each bowl with 1 stuffed chicken breast and serve hot.

PER SERVING   Calories: 548 | Fat: 10.0 grams | Protein: 56.5 grams | Sodium: 2843 milligrams | Fiber: 5.1 grams | Carbohydrates: 56.9 grams | Sugar: 19.2 grams

POWER SOURCES

SPINACH: vitamin K supports the immune system

GARLIC: anti-inflammatory compounds target arteries to reduce the incidence of blockages

TOMATO: vitamin C combats free-radical damage

Roasted Red Pepper Hummus with Spicy Sweet Potato Chips

Prep Time: 15 minutes | **Cook Time:** 40 minutes | **Serves 2**

1 small red bell pepper, halved lengthwise and seeded

1 tablespoon plus ½ cup olive oil, divided

1 large sweet potato, thinly sliced (preferably with a mandoline)

2 tablespoons coconut oil, divided

1 teaspoon salt

½ teaspoon cayenne

1 teaspoon garlic powder

1 cup canned, rinsed, and drained chickpeas

POWER SOURCES

SWEET POTATO: vitamin A promotes blood health by increasing iron absorption

BELL PEPPER: lutein and zeaxanthin prevent cataract development

CHICKPEAS: protein is essential for energy production and use

1   Preheat oven to 425°F and place red pepper halves flesh-side up on a baking sheet. Drizzle with 1 tablespoon olive oil and bake for 5–10 minutes or until flesh is cooked thoroughly. Remove from baking sheet and set aside.

2   Place sweet potato in a bowl or plastic Ziploc bag. Drizzle sweet potato slices with 1 tablespoon coconut oil and shake or mix to coat all slices.

3   Grease the baking sheet with remaining 1 tablespoon coconut oil. Layer half of the sweet potato slices evenly on the baking sheet without overlapping.

4   Bake until slightly crisp, about 10 minutes. Flip sweet potato slices; bake for 5–10 minutes until browned and crisp. Remove from heat and place on paper towels to absorb excess moisture; sprinkle with salt and cayenne. Repeat for remaining sweet potato slices.

5   In a large blender, add the roasted red peppers, garlic powder, and chickpeas and blend on high until emulsified. Drizzle in remaining ½ cup olive oil gradually while blending.

6   Pour half of hummus mixture into each of two serving bowls and top each with half of the sweet potato chips. Serve warm or cooled.

PER SERVING   Calories: 1134 | Fat: 112.8 grams | Protein: 6.0 grams | Sodium: 1327 milligrams | Fiber: 5.5 grams | Carbohydrates: 21.4 grams | Sugar: 4.3 grams

Creamy Broccoli Soup

Prep Time: 5 minutes | **Cook Time:** 10 minutes | **Serves 2**

1 cup almond milk

8 ounces silken tofu

4 cups broccoli spears

1 small yellow onion, peeled and chopped

4 garlic cloves, chopped

2 teaspoons salt

¼ teaspoon cayenne

¼ cup nonfat yogurt

¼ teaspoon cracked black pepper

1. In a large pot over medium-high heat, combine almond milk, tofu, broccoli, onion, garlic, salt, and cayenne. Cook until broccoli and onion are fork-tender, about 10 minutes. Remove from heat.

2. Using an immersion blender, blend on high until all ingredients are fully broken down and thoroughly combined, about 5 minutes.

3. Pour equal amounts of soup into each of two serving bowls. Garnish each bowl with ⅛ cup yogurt and ⅛ teaspoon cracked black pepper. Serve hot or cold.

PER SERVING   Calories: 327 | Fat: 12.2 grams | Protein: 27.3 grams | Sodium: 2509 milligrams | Fiber: 11.0 grams | Carbohydrates: 34.4 grams | Sugar: 11.4 grams

POWER SOURCES

BROCCOLI: vitamin C assists in iron absorption

ONION: quercetin helps to safeguard cells against free-radical damage

GARLIC: allicin combats dangerous triglycerides and cholesterol levels

YOGURT: B vitamins support muscle contractions

U.S./Metric Conversion Chart

VOLUME CONVERSIONS

U.S. Volume Measure	Metric Equivalent
⅛ teaspoon	0.5 milliliter
¼ teaspoon	1 milliliter
½ teaspoon	2 milliliters
1 teaspoon	5 milliliters
½ tablespoon	7 milliliters
1 tablespoon (3 teaspoons)	15 milliliters
2 tablespoons (1 fluid ounce)	30 milliliters
¼ cup (4 tablespoons)	60 milliliters
⅓ cup	90 milliliters
½ cup (4 fluid ounces)	125 milliliters
⅔ cup	160 milliliters
¾ cup (6 fluid ounces)	180 milliliters
1 cup (16 tablespoons)	250 milliliters
1 pint (2 cups)	500 milliliters
1 quart (4 cups)	1 liter (about)

WEIGHT CONVERSIONS

U.S. Weight Measure	Metric Equivalent
½ ounce	15 grams
1 ounce	30 grams
2 ounces	60 grams
3 ounces	85 grams
¼ pound (4 ounces)	115 grams
½ pound (8 ounces)	225 grams
¾ pound (12 ounces)	340 grams
1 pound (16 ounces)	454 grams

OVEN TEMPERATURE CONVERSIONS

Degrees Fahrenheit	Degrees Celsius
200 degrees F	95 degrees C
250 degrees F	120 degrees C
275 degrees F	135 degrees C
300 degrees F	150 degrees C
325 degrees F	160 degrees C
350 degrees F	180 degrees C
375 degrees F	190 degrees C
400 degrees F	205 degrees C
425 degrees F	220 degrees C
450 degrees F	230 degrees C

BAKING PAN SIZES

American	Metric
8 x 1½ inch round baking pan	20 x 4 cm cake tin
9 x 1½ inch round baking pan	23 x 3.5 cm cake tin
11 x 7 x 1½ inch baking pan	28 x 18 x 4 cm baking tin
13 x 9 x 2 inch baking pan	30 x 20 x 5 cm baking tin
2 quart rectangular baking dish	30 x 20 x 3 cm baking tin
15 x 10 x 2 inch baking pan	30 x 25 x 2 cm baking tin (Swiss roll tin)
9 inch pie plate	22 x 4 or 23 x 4 cm pie plate
7 or 8 inch springform pan	18 or 20 cm springform or loose bottom cake tin
9 x 5 x 3 inch loaf pan	23 x 13 x 7 cm or 2 lb narrow loaf or pate tin
1½ quart casserole	1.5 liter casserole
2 quart casserole	2 liter casserole

Index